Handbook of Management Tactics

Handbook of Management Tactics

Aggressive Strategies for Getting Things Done YOUR Way

Richard H. Buskirk

HAWTHORN BOOKS, INC.
Publishers/NEW YORK

HANDBOOK OF MANAGEMENT TACTICS
(previously published as *Handbook of Managerial Tactics*)

 All inquiries should be addressed to Cahners Books, Inc., 221 Columbus Avenue, Boston, Mass. 02116. This book was manufactured in the United States of America and published simultaneously in Canada by Prentice-Hall of Canada, Limited, 1870 Birchmount Road, Scarborough, Ontario.

Published by arrangement with Cahners Books, Inc.

Library of Congress Catalog Card Number: 77-70138

ISBN: 0-8015-3489-5

1 2 3 4 5 6 7 8 9 10

Contents

Foreword *by Jerry Della Femina* xi

Preface xv

Introduction xviii

1 The Importance of Tactics 1

Difficulty of Selecting Tactics 10
Factors to Consider in Tactical Decisions 10
How to Learn 17
Proper Use of Tactics 20
Terminology of Presentation 21
A Final Word on Keeping Your Perspective 22

2 Operating Tactics 23

The Choice of Tactics—Which Road to Travel 25
Never, But Never, Wound a King 27
The Fait Accompli—The Accomplished Fact 29
Sandbagging 31
Avoid Battle 34
Choose Your Battleground 35
Be Present on the Battleground 37

Make Certain Preparations are Complete Before Battle 40
Touch All Bases 41
Personalize 42
Hold Your Coat 44
Frontal Attack 45
The Steam Roller—The Power Play 48
Outflank 'Em! 49
Throw Your Own Party 50
One-On-One 51
Muddling Through 54
Divide and Conquer 55
Marshal Your Forces or Turn Out the Guard 58
Aim at Strength 60
Aim at Weakness 62
Run for Daylight 63
Speed 64
Jump on the Bandwagon 65
The Trap Play 67
Harass 69
Get Lost! 70
Give 'em a Flat Tire to Run On 71
Let Them Furnish Their Own Rope 72
Push 'em Off the Dock 74
Use a Hatchet Man 75
Don't Burn Your Bridges Behind You 77
. . . Leave the Door Open 79
Surrender Quickly 80
Run For Cover 81
Clear Out 83
Fold the Enterprise 84
Be the Fall Guy 85
Subvert 86

Let Them Set Their Own Sentences 87
Righteous Indignation 88
Silence—Maintain Confidence 89
Take the Pitch 91
Act, Don't React 92
Don't Act From Emotion 94
Test the Water 95
Laugh it Off 96
Ignore the Static 97
Die on the Vine 99
Let 'em Bitch 100
The Hot Potato 101
Innocent All the Way 103
Piggyback 104
Put it in Writing 105
Do Something, No Matter What 106
Go See the Wizard 107
Let's Do Research 109
Keep A Key 111
Refer to a Committee 112
Have a Fall Guy 114
Control the Environment—Bestow the Status Symbols 115
Exile to Siberia 116
Conclusion 118

3 Tactics Involving Personal Relationships some people call it politics 119

Loyalty 124
Work 126

Avoid Losers 128
Put Salve on Their Wounds 129
Pour Oil on Troubled Waters 130

4 Timing Tactics 133

Leave Well Enough Alone 138
Choose Your Time 140
Be Patient 142
Let the Situation Worsen 143
Strike While the Iron is Hot 144
Strike When You're Strong 145
All Bets are Made on the First Tee 147
Strike When it Hurts the Adversaries 148
Don't Let Them Dig In 149
Grab It Now 150

5 Negotiating and Persuasive Tactics 153

Narrowing the Field 158
Step-by-Step 159
The Blank Check 160
Bait Your Hook 162
Disguise True Desires 163
Be Your Own Casting Director 164
Carry a Big Stick 165
Bring Your Own Expert 167

Set Up Straw Men 168
Nose in the Tent or Foot in the Door 169
Leave the Lid on Pandora's Box 170
Shoot for the Moon 172
Raise the Stakes—Buy the Pot 173
Learn the Adversary's Limits 174
Run a Bluff 176
Keep the Trump Card 178
The Documented Lie 178
The Red Herring 180
Be Unreasonable 181
Keep Talking 182
Keep Quiet 183
Stall 184
Capitalize on Defeat 186
Waltz Them to the Courthouse Steps 187
The Grapevine 190
Take a Vote 191
Force the Issue 192
Listen 193
Make Them Think They've Won 194
Avoid Personalities 195
Plant the Seed 197
Where the Body's Buried—Blackmail 198
Pay 'Em Off 199
White Hat—Black Hat 202
Hitch a Lie to a Truth 203
Make the Future Look More Expensive 205
Salting the Mine 206
The Architect's Window 208

Set the Hook 209
Establish Expertise Early 211
How Does the Land Lie? 213

6 **Some Tactical Problems and how they were handled or mishandled 215**

C. C. and the Boston Shootout 217
Charles and the Runaway Committee 219
Rickie—an Insecure Employee 221
Dan 223
The Lease 225
The Two Bosses 229
Settling Debts 232
The Fence 235
The Major League Tryout 236
High Draft Choice for Green Bay 238
The Lure 241

Foreword

When I first got into business, I met a man whom I shall call Gregory. Gregory was riding high in those days. He was vice-president and creative director of a large $100 million advertising agency, and the only threat to his empire was Ed, a young copy supervisor, who was one of his trusted lieutenants.

Young Ed was good. Very good. He played the game beautifully. Lunch every two weeks with Gregory's boss, Mr. Powell, the beautiful agency president. Ed would never criticize his boss, Gregory, outright. Ed would simply say, "Good old Greg. You can't beat him from keeping the troops' morale up. At 5:00 P.M. anybody from the cleaning lady on up is pulled into his office for a drink."

To this, Mr. Powell, the beautiful agency president, would smile like a Cheshire cat and make a mental note. "So young Ed is telling me that Gregory is drinking too much." Sometimes, Ed would address the agency's creative review board and say things like, "I want you to know that the new creative concept for Frizzbee toothpaste is Gregory's and Gregory's alone. The man is a genius. Last week as he was running out to catch the 5:45 to Connecticut, he yelled to me over his shoulder, 'Let's say Frizzbee toothpaste contains a new tooth-whitening ingredient called Pakistan. Okay, Ed, now you get some monkeys to execute it.' And without breaking his stride, Gregory was out the door. What a genius."

Of course, the creative review board sitting there listening to Ed didn't think too much of Pakistan as a miracle ingredient or Gregory for thinking about it. And when Mr. Powell, the beautiful agency president, heard Ed's little speech he thought, "So Gregory isn't paying much attention to his job these days and he's relying on good old Ed to make excuses for him."

Soon everybody at the agency felt that it was a matter of days if not hours until Ed would get Gregory's job. They also wondered how Gregory can be so trusting and so stupid. He was letting Ed love him to death. And then one day it happened.

One Monday morning on each employee's desk there was a simple four line memo which said, "It is with a great deal of regret that I must announce the resignation of Ed _____. Ed has been a trusted and valued co-worker for the past five years and I'm sure we all wish him well on any future endeavors." The memo was signed Gregory _____.

What a switch. Young Ed had been fired. It all had come to a boil the previous Friday when young Ed felt he was strong enough to make his move for the top job. He privately met and lined up on his side every member of the creative review board. Then he made the decision. Mr. Powell, the beautiful agency president, was going to be on his side. And so he would talk to him first thing Monday morning and explain to him why he, Ed, should be the new creative director. Unfortunately, what happened was somebody squealed. Somebody told Gregory that on Monday morning he was going to get fired. Gregory simply picked up the phone and called Charlie, the president of Crashem Cars, the agency's largest account.

And so on Saturday, Mr. Powell, the beautiful agency president, found himself playing golf with Gregory, his creative director, and Charlie, his client. As Charlie was teeing off on the 16th hole, Gregory leaned over and whispered to Mr. Powell, "I think I am going to have to let young Ed go. He is a troublemaker who might say something and lose the agency my good, good, good friend Charlie's Crashem Cars account." "Sh, sh, sh," said Mr. Powell, "he'll hear you." "I'll fire him tomorrow," said Gregory. "I'll call him when he gets home from church."

One day, years later, when we were both enjoying a three-martini, two-bottle-of-wine lunch, I asked Gregory about young

Ed. "Jerry," he said, "young Ed really thought he was a Machiavellian character. If he had worked it so that I was fired that Friday instead of letting the weekend go by, he would be creative director today. But the schmuck probably only read half of Machiavelli's *The Prince*. It's a cinch he never read page 97." "Page 97?" I said. "What does it say?" With this, Greg took a long satisfied puff on a cigar, leaned back, smiled, and said, "It says 'never wound a king.' "

Is *The Handbook of Management Tactics* an honest account of what goes on in the business world? Yes, definitely yes. Will most businessmen admit this? No, definitely no. And yet I submit that there isn't a single man who has reached the top in business who hasn't at one time or another lived the life, every page, every chapter, every thought, represented here.

I showed the manuscript of this book to a friend of mine who is known as the most gentle, most respected man in his business. "Bullshit," he roared. "Pure bullshit. I don't believe a word of it." "Jack," I said, "why don't you sit back and think for one second about how you got to the top when so many of your friends failed." He thought for a minute and then said, "Son of a bitch, I'm so good at it that I don't even tell myself I'm doing it."

Jerry Della Femina

Preface

Some sensitive souls will be needlessly disturbed by the tactics discussed in this book. They will feel that somehow it is immoral even to study the subject of management tactics, let alone use them. So let us get this matter of ethics out in the open right now.

First, nowhere in this book is the use of any one tactic either recommended or not recommended—each is just presented for your information. You are the sole determinant of how you will use this information.

Second, there is nothing unethical about knowledge. Knowing about sin does not a sinner make—sin requires action.

Third, a tactic by itself is neither good nor bad. Ethical questions can only be raised about how a tactic is used. Many people might claim that it is unquestionably unethical to lie, but there are situations in which the truth would do harm while a lie would do good. Try telling a rejected job applicant that the reason for his rejection is that his intellect leaves something to be desired. Sugar coat it as you might try, it would still come out, "You're too stupid for the job!" Now what good has been done by the alleged truth? Another tactic, admittedly a more deceptive one, would be not only wiser, but kinder.

Fourth, there is no way to avoid using tactics, some tactics. Tactics are the means by which managers do their jobs, execute their plans. They must use them. The question is not whether one should or should not use tactics; rather, it is whether one should use this tactic or that one. An ineffective tactic is not more moral, more ethical, than an effective one; yet that is the essence of the argument put forth by some critics of management tactics who seem bent on restricting managers to the use of only ineffective tools. And that is what tactics are—the manager's tools.

No claim is made that this compilation of management tactics is exhaustive, for it most certainly is not. You are encouraged to add to it your favorite management ploys—most executives have them. Instead, this book is intended to introduce you to tactical thinking and to give you some insights into many of the more common tactics that you may encounter.

Admittedly, some of the tactics are closely related, but they are split into separate categories when the tactics differ in some significant way or intent.

An earlier attempt to include some of this material in a book on management was met with great hostility by reviewers, who maintained, "People shouldn't be taught such things. It isn't proper to speak of these matters, even if they are true. There are things that must be learned the hard way." Nonsense! I see little virtue in learning anything the hard way if it can be learned in an easier manner. Admittedly there are many lessons that evidently can be learned only the "hard way," but it seems that they are assimilated more quickly if one has been properly prepared for them.

Several top executives of rather large companies read this manuscript and encouraged me to publish it. I would like to thank them publicly for their helpful comments, but they said they would sue if I mentioned them by name. The able tactician prefers to remain unrecognized.

As usual, the real work on this book was done by my able assistant, Sylvia Arnot, who said that she wouldn't sue. This is an example of the give recognition where due tactic, used far too seldom.

Richard Buskirk

Introduction

Certain managerial terms—such as objectives, goals, strategies, tactics, and policies—have been used so frequently by so many different writers that an understandable confusion exists about them. In particular, the terms "strategies" and "tactics" are frequently misunderstood. A strategy is a plan of action an administrator develops to achieve some goal, which can be either personal or organizational.

Tactics are the *behavioral maneuverings* a manager undertakes to carry out his strategies. In military parlance, tactics are the maneuvering of men and machines to carry out a plan. A general may develop a strategy for winning a battle and then have his staff develop appropriate tactics to execute it. Indeed, a war itself may be but a tactic in some overall political strategy. Tactics are used at all levels; they are simply behavior designed to carry out a plan of action.

In a very real sense all behavior is tactical; that is, everything the individual does can be considered some sort of tactic. Seldom does one consciously consider them such, for most of our behavior is so routine, so programmed, that we give little thought to it. We just do it. We do the things that have yielded us satisfactory results in the past. We are conditioned to behavior that works, to tactics that work.

Perhaps the word "tactics" smacks too much of the military, thus causing some discomfort, but it need not. The term is used here to denote the behavioral maneuverings of the individual who is attempting to carry out some plan—trying to do something. Tactics are what you *do* in carrying out some plan you have in mind. We all use tactics, both consciously and unconsciously. You want to play poker with the boys Thursday night, so you take your wife out for dinner in an attempt to exercise the tactic, "Quid Pro Quo"—tit for tat. And no doubt you have been victimized many times by the tactics of others. Perhaps a subordinate who wanted to do something of which you disapproved just did it and presented you with a *fait accompli*. There is no end to the list of examples of tactics that you use and that are used upon you daily. In a manner of speaking, just about all behavior involves tactics. The mother next door comes over for a face-to-face encounter with your wife concerning the misbehavior of your seven-year-old son—a one-on-one encounter. So it goes.

So this book is concerned with how to go about doing what ever it is you want to do. It is hoped that it will cause you to think a bit about how best to accomplish your plans.

1

The Importance of Tactics

Publishers of books such as this one have a quaint tactic of sending them to various noted writers in the same field for quotes about the book that can be used in promotional releases.

Peter Drucker's unpromotable comment was, "Tactics bore me. I am only interested in strategy." To this, my unworthy reaction was, "I am sorry, Dr. Drucker, but strategy is not really the address of success. Rather, it can be better found living in the house of tactics."

Observe that companies in the same industry follow a wide variety of strategies with success. Moreover, companies using strategies identical to those of successful firms can fail. The difference—how well they tactically implement their strategies.

Note the different strategies used by cosmetic companies. Avon goes door-to-door; Revlon and others use extensive distribution supported by large promotional efforts; Charles of the Ritz uses exclusive department store outlets; some products are marketed as medical aids while others are but fads for teenagers. All of these examples are viable strategies whose success depends upon tactical execution. While Revlon's basic strategy is focused around advertising, its success depends upon how well that advertising campaign is executed. Whether or not the ads sell the goods depends upon how well hundreds of people do their jobs—the models, the photographers, the layout men, the copywriters, etc.

The world's greatest football strategist will be a loser if his lads fail to block and tackle with skill and vigor. And with sufficient skill and vigor, strategy is simple—á la Vince Lombardi, knock 'em down and run past 'em!

It is a sorrowful thing to observe, but many fine strategies with highly desirable goals have failed for want of proper tactics. A sales manager formulated a new compensation plan designed to increase both sales and the employee's earnings—worthy goals. But he gave no thought to tactics; he tried a direct frontal attack, but was soundly defeated by the men who were afraid of his new plan. Other tactics could have carried the day.

Indeed, many ill-advised strategies have been effected successfully through the use of excellent tactics. One college administrator had developed an organizational plan he wanted adopted. Unfortunately, it was a bad plan, as subsequent events made painfully obvious. However, through adept tactical moves he overcame the opposition that could have easily sidetracked his plan. And so it may be that the successful execution of plans depends more on the tactics employed than upon their intrinsic soundness, a most lamentable circumstance. Therefore, it behooves the developer of sound plans to become tactically adept so that his ideas can compete successfully with inferior ones. Many talented young executives are thwarted in their ambitions because they operate under the naive assumption that right is might. Unfortunately, they are frequently done in by people of lesser talents who are more adept tactically. It is insufficient to devise wise strategies if they are not implemented with the proper tactics.

Perhaps the most famous tactical blunder in our times will prove to be the Watergate affair. Most able tacticians shudder at the total managerial incompetence shown by the people involved in that disgraceful episode of American history. Assuming that the general plan was to reelect Nixon and have him conduct a successful presidency, it is difficult to comprehend how anyone could fit the tactic of bugging the Democratic headquarters and all of the subsequent mismanagement into that plan. In the Watergate affair, there were thousands of separate tactics involved because there were numerous acts committed by many people. There was the burglary and the culprits' apprehension. Then there were all the actions connected with the coverup and the many tactical decisions made by the participants. For example, why in the world would any attorney general in his right mind even think about listening to the nonsense that was being put before him in his own office by Liddy? Mitchell's subordinates should have known better than to ever involve him in such affairs. Endless questions can be asked about the tactics chosen by everyone concerned, but, of course, there are no answers except that the tactics quite obviously didn't work. And, after all, one measure of the wisdom with which a tactic is chosen is—does it work?

Consider a different type of managerial breakdown. The president of a large university was unexpectedly asked to resign (he was fired) by the board of trustees, much to the chagrin of the faculty with whom he was as popular as a college president can expect to be. No reasons were publicly given, thus much fuss was made all over campus about the incident, but to no avail. What finally emerged from investigations was that the president was fired because he made two tactical blunders, both of which had the same goal—they were designed or would have resulted in bestowing far more power upon himself. This particular university had an exceptionally large board of trustees; therefore, it was not an effective ruling body. So it had created an executive board of a few powerful trustees to oversee the operations of the university. The executive board took an active part in setting policies. The president, after about a year in office, undertook to change the organizational structure of the university in such a way that the executive board would be disbanded, ostensibly so that power would revert to the larger body. However, no management-wise individual was going to be fooled by that move. It would be impossible for the larger body to play an active role in the management of the institution. Thus, the president would be left with more freedom to run things as he desired. His move was interpreted by the members of the executive board as a power grab. They reacted swiftly and decisively to the threat by immediately polling the entire board and getting its permission to ask for the president's resignation, which was soon forthcoming.

The other tactical blunder the president had made was to expel a long-time, respected institute from the campus without having a convincing reason for doing so. This act upset many powerful people who were supporters of the institute. In short, the president made two tactical moves that threatened the institutional power structure, but he lacked a sufficient power base from which to operate. The result was catastrophe. He had not accurately assessed the situation.

Let's examine a career that turned to dust because of tactical blundering. Ed became dean of the college of liberal arts at a major university. He was a visionary who wanted to shake college education out of its doldrums by instituting some new educational methods. Since it was a private university, fund raising was one of Ed's major responsibilities and he was particularly adept at it. He spent most of his time raising money. He had little contact with his faculty, particularly the heads of his various departments, who were people he disdained. He was dissatisfied with their talents, but he refrained from removing them from their positions, even though he had the power to do so. He felt that by making as few changes as possible during the first two years he would stir up little resistance to the new programs he was instituting. In carrying out his plans he would simply create the new institutes by adding them to the existing structure, thus eliminating the necessity of gaining departmental approval for his actions. Finally, when the time came for reorganizing the whole school, he thought he would be particularly clever and appoint some of his enemies—the old, established, full professors who, by this time, were alienated because they had so little contact with the man—to a committee responsible for the reorganization. The committee met for a period of several months and finally issued its report. Its sole recommendation for the reorganization of the school was for the dean to resign. As a body the group walked to the president's office with its recommendation, and for reasons known only by the top administration it was accepted. The man was forced out.

His tactics were horrible. They could not have been better selected by his worst enemies. Instead, he should have first established communications with his faculty, particularly his department heads. If he did not like his department heads, then he should have managed to get them out of their positions, but in any case he should not have ignored them. He just had not spent enough time on the battlefield to know what was going on. Second, the idea of appointing his enemies to a committee to make recommendations about his organization seems, on the surface, the height of folly; for once they had created a document, he had something with which he had to cope. He certainly could not have expected his enemies to come forth with anything he was going to like. Thus he automatically created a situation in which he was going to have to fight his senior men, a most unfortunate tactical blunder. If he had followed wiser tactics, he would have his job today and the institution would be much the better for it. He had done many good things during his short stay.

Another illustrative tactical blunder is the Mazda incident. The Japanese had placed a great deal of power in the hands of an American by the name of Brown, who headed up the Mazda automobile operation in the United States. The car, because it was unique and particularly well made, had a phenomenal initial success. The market liked it. Then the government bureaucrats made a terrible blunder which was devastating to Mazda. The EPA, in measuring gas mileage, used the same techniques on the Mazda, a car powered by a rotary engine, as it did on the piston engine cars. The results were grossly in error. Where the EPA registered the Mazda mileage at a little over nine miles per gallon, the fact was that most Mazda drivers were reporting over

22 miles per gallon on the road. These government results were given wide publicity by the press and they hurt Mazda sales badly. The president had two choices. First, he could ignore the whole thing and let word of mouth counter the government; because after all, a great deal of government information comes out that people do not pay much attention to. Witness the warnings on cigarette packages as a prime example of this type of foolishness. Word of mouth is a powerful device. The fact was that the Mazda cars were fine devices that were proving themselves in the field.

Or Brown could fight the government's findings. He chose the latter tactic—to go to war. He challenged the EPA. Once a bureaucrat is challenged and called incompetent, he must defend himself. Somehow Brown was outmaneuvered in the retesting, for the retests came up with the same results, thus reinforcing the first reports to the even greater detriment of Mazda sales. Mazda had failed to get the government to change its basic testing procedures. Mazda was playing in a game in which the deck was stacked against their car. Though what the government did to that company was a terrible thing, it was brought on by the inept tactics of Mazda management. At the time of this writing Mazda still is having difficulties.

We have been looking at failures; now let's look at a tactical success.

A venture capitalist was selling one of his enterprises to a corporation formed by three young men, all of whom were financially well off from inherited wealth. The lawyers had arranged for the capitalist to sell his corporation to the young men's corporation for a small down payment and a very large note. In turn, one of the young men had promised to buy the note personally from the capitalist, thus giving him all of his money. The buyers' tax people had reasons why they wanted to execute the sale in this manner, or so they said. Moreover, they did not want the personal sale of the note made part of the contract of sale because it might jeopardize the tax game they were trying to play. It was not known what was going on in their heads, but that was the way the deal had to take place. After the transaction, the seller presented the note to the young man for purchase but was told that the situation had changed. The young man was now unable to buy the note. The seller had been bamboozled, but he did not panic because he had made some observations of the lad's behavior. He had his tactic ready to use. First, he sold the note with recourse to his banker and notified the maker of the assignment. The thought behind this tactic was to have the maker pay the bank not the seller. People are intimidated by banks and are more likely to pay a bank than an individual. Moreover, he wanted the note at the bank in order to establish the facts. He wanted credible witnesses. He instructed the banker to notify him immediately if for any reason payment on the note was not made on time. The terms of the discounting at the bank required the capitalist to pay the bank if the maker of the note failed to do so. Moreover, the note contained an acceleration clause which clearly stated that if any payment was not paid on time the entire note became due immediately along with attorney's fees. Furthermore, the sales contract was specifically drawn to state that time was of the essence in all payments.

The capitalist had noted many flaws in the character of the buyers, among which was a certain tardiness in everything they did. He was confident that they would not make their payments on time. Sure enough, when the first payment came due on November 1, it was missed, so the capitalist went to the bank and paid off the whole note. Then he called his lawyer and had him make demand for the total amount of the note because it was in default. On November 8, one of the young men tried to pay the capitalist the monthly payment despite the fact that he had been notified by the bank of the circumstances. The capitalist said, "John, I think you'd better talk to your attorney," and refused the payment. Had he touched the money it would have been a tactical and legal blunder. When the buyers finally realized what was going on they were furious, as were their attorneys, but there was not a thing they could do about it. They had to pay the note as was promised in the first place, all as a result of good tactics on the part of the venture capitalist. In essence, he had squeezed money from a bunch of fast operators because of their inept tactics. Had they made the payments on time there would have been nothing the man could have done to accelerate the receipt of his money.

Difficulty of Selecting Tactics

While you might wonder why all these people chose tactics that were seemingly so poor for the accomplishment of what they wanted to do, you should appreciate that when one is actually making a tactical decision, he many times not only fails to see all of the options open to him, but also lacks needed information. Moreover, even the best of tacticians frequently make mistakes, either because they were unaware of some factors or had misjudged them. Thus, we should spend some time talking about the various factors that affect tactical decisions.

Factors to Consider in Tactical Decisions

No significance should be attached to the order of discussion of the following factors. It is just a laundry list of things one might consider.

Personality of the Other Party—The Adversary

Suppose that you work for a boss who is permissive, tolerant, and easy going—one who judges you by your results. Under such circumstances you might feel that a *fait accompli* would be a good tactic to use in certain situations. However, if your boss is highly authoritarian and jealous of his managerial prerogatives, your job might be in jeopardy if you use the same tactic. Clearly, the personality and philosophy of the other party will determine that person's reactions to your tactics.

Bill was a fussy type who continually harrassed his subordinates with minor complaints. The tactic most subordinates used in dealing with him was to ignore the static. They knew him well—he only wanted to make noise and be noticed. He was trying to act like a boss, but he was powerless to rectify any of the things about which he complained. Moreover, his people doubted whether he really gave much thought to what he said.

Another important factor to assess is the aggressiveness or hostility of the other person. Some people react strongly to some tactics being used upon them, while others are placid. Clearly, you can be more adventuresome tactically when dealing with placid personalities than you can with an aggressive, hostile individual. Recall the corporate sale and note situation described previously? Those tactics were based upon an assessment of the personalities of the other parties. The seller of the business expected the other people to be late in making their payments and arranged to get his money based upon that knowledge.

In deciding whether or not to go one-on-one with an individual, it is important that you assess the compatibility of your personalities. It might be a mistake to have a direct confrontation with people who are incompatible with you. Police maintain that one of the underlying reasons for many shootings is that a person confronts someone else whose personality leans toward the violent. The adversary's reaction is to get a gun and do something with it. That really was not what the tactician had in mind at all when he started the affair.

Perhaps one of the errors Nixon made in his handling of the Watergate fiasco was that he badly misjudged the resolution and determination of his enemies to get rid of him by exploiting that episode. Perhaps he thought it would go away if he stalled, but it did not. They would not let it die. Normally, if one can stall long enough, conflicts may die a natural death; people just become bored with the matter.

Power Base—Yours and Theirs

Some tactics require the possession of a certain amount of power for successful execution. You simply cannot use them unless you have the power to do so. As a general rule, people have less power than they believe. A young basketball coach of seemingly great talent took over a team whose record had been particularly miserable. He immediately instituted a highly authoritarian regime that chased off all but seven players. He did not have enough players left to hold a scrimmage. His tactics were based upon having power to force the players to do his bidding—do what I say or I'll kick you off the team. This tactic did not work, because not playing on that team was not a threat that held much fear for the players. He badly misjudged his power base. The athletic director relieved him of his duties at the end of the year.

Even in the highest echelons, executives often badly misjudge their power. A particularly aggressive and imaginative man took over the presidency of a failing agricultural implements manufacturer. He had great plans for revitalizing its dealerships and promotional programs. He immediately began executing his plans with effective tactics, but in the process he misjudged how much power the board of directors had bestowed upon him. They asked for his resignation when a significant faction of the board became fearful of his actions. He was just too forceful for them. When you have an adequate power base, you can try many tactics directly. Without a power base you are forced to use more clever, indirect tactics. The power you have will determine, to a large extent, the tactics you will use. Thus you must have an accurate perception of your power; a great deal of grief lies in store for the individual who overestimates his power. It is far safer to underestimate than to overestimate your power, even though an underestimation at times does cause you some unnecessary maneuverings.

Time Requirement

Some tactics require more time to execute than others. If you are in a rush, if the situation requires fast action that precludes time-consuming, devious maneuvers, then you may be forced to use faster, more direct tactics. There is simply not time to do it the preferable way.

Hal had an excellent job, but suddenly was offered a much better one in another city. The nature of the situation required that Hal make a decision on the offer within two weeks, despite the fact that he would have liked to have stalled for a month or so to better evaluate some developments at the place he was working. The stall tactic was precluded by the time demands of the situation. Hal could not play the game he wanted to and should have played.

Your Values

Unquestionably, your personal values, preferences, likes, and dislikes should play an important role in the tactics you use. As you read about the various tactics described in the remainder of the book you will no doubt feel uncomfortable about some of them. You would not like using them; they are not you. That is fine and the way things should be. There is absolutely no thought that you should blindly use all of the tactics mentioned in this book, for it is impossible to write anything of this nature that would appeal to everyone.

Wynn tried to use the documented lie tactic in his dealings with the IRS, but unfortunately he was not a very good liar. His heart was not in it. He was not at all comfortable—a fact that soon became evident to the IRS agent, who immediately pounced upon him. It was the wrong tactic for Wynn to use. He should not have used it, because it was against his nature to do so.

The Stakes—How Important is the Plan?

If you were sitting in a poker game and the pot was small, it would not be wise to try to bluff your way to victory by risking a good portion of your poke. Normally, one bluffs only when the stakes are sufficiently high to make winning worth the risk. In business most wise executives forego an open confrontation with adversaries except when the stakes are sufficiently high and no other tactics seem effective. One cannot go through life fighting over every little matter. It runs counter to the tactic "Save Your Ammunition." Perhaps the Watergate conspirators were tempted into their shenanigans because of the size of the stakes. But that is hardly an excuse, because the very size of the stakes was the reason they should have been far more careful in their selection of tactics. It was a matter of what they would gain by successfully completing the burglary, versus what they stood to lose if caught. The gain/loss ratio was grossly inadequate.

When the stakes are high and the going gets rough, even the most worldly of business people can be appalled at what people will do. Look at the tactics used by the management of Equity Funding in trying to keep their positions when the company was not doing well. They lied, cheated, stole, and misrepresented the facts concerning the company. True, some of them ended up in jail, but only years after the tactics had been executed. Seldom do the tacticians, at the time of making decisions which involve high stakes, consider possible legal penalties. The pain of failure is immediate, whereas the pain of the law is greatly discounted because it lies somewhere in the distant future as a remote possibility.

Thus, when you are involved in a high-stakes situation do not be surprised at the tactics your adversary may use against you. Be prepared for anything.

Your Talents

The execution of some tactics may be beyond one's skills. The person who endeavors to persuade other people to do his bidding by meeting with them *one-on-one* assumes that he has the personal persuasive skills to get the job done. Many times that is not a valid assumption.

One can not very well raise the stakes and thus buy the pot if he does not have the necessary money for the action.

Several tactics require that the user possess some ability at hiding his true emotions, his true feelings about the matter at hand. There are people who are unable to do this.

Possible Repercussions

In many situations the possible repercussions from the tactics used are trivial and can thus be ignored. As you enter the house after a long, arduous day's work your spouse levels a blast at your forgetfulness—you did not bring home any milk. You instinctively *surrender quickly*, having learned the hard way that other tactics are doomed to failure. Relax! You're safe. No repercussions will be forthcoming.

However, as you walk into a customer's office the next day, he crawls all over you for some difficulties with the last shipment. It would be easy to surrender quickly, thus avoiding more conflict. However, to do so might obligate the firm to do something for which it might not really be liable. The wiser person considers the possible repercussions of his actions. In this matter, the salesperson stalled by saying, "Let me find out what the facts are and get back to you on it."

In all candor, there are also situations in which the opposite tactics should be used. If you stall, the customer becomes angry. Surrender and little damage can be done to you.

The dean who appointed a committee of his enemies to reorganize his school failed to consider the possible repercussions of setting up what amounted to a runaway grand jury.

The present-day tactics of the oil producing and exporting countries (OPEC) in pricing oil may have some interesting long-run repercussions on those nations.

One of the difficulties with most of the tactics selected by our politicians and bureaucrats is that they are short-run moves largely based on political expediency. But all of our national problems are so loaded with emotional content and are so sensitive politically that direct tactics to solve them are not feasible.

Ease of Use

Some tactics are easy to use while others are not. It is easy to be honest and straight-forward, but waltzing one's opponent to the courthouse steps can take some doing. Bluffing is not easy and it takes some effort to document a lie. If you plan to use a hatchet man, then you must either have one available or get one. It is easy to ignore the static but more difficult to take a positive action on something.

Obviously, simple, easy tactics have great virtue. The more complicated tactics pose larger risks and require more effort. One might be tempted to propose the principle that one should use the easy tactic unless there is good reason not to do so.

However, there is a problem with such a principle. The lazy

tactician is sorely tempted to use the easy tactic in all situations even though it is many times the wrong one.

Our national bureaucrats, for example can only defend many of their tactics on the grounds that they were the easiest tactics they could use. A well-bred bureaucrat opts for the easy way out of a situation. He disdains any tactic that contains risk to his position or requires too much effort. It was much easier to establish a nationwide speed limit of 55 mph than to make intelligent adjustments for driving conditions. A speed of 55 mph is easily accepted in congested eastern areas where the driver is going only a few miles, but it is something else again in the west where the driver is going several hundred miles over barren desert. But no matter. One law! That is the easiest tactic to execute.

How To Learn

Learning tactical adroitness is not easy. First, one's tactical development is facilitated if his work and/or social activities bring him into sufficiently close contact with a variety of managers that he can observe true tactical behavior and its results. Tactics are difficult to learn through third parties, because the distortion introduced by them frequently makes the messages misleading. Some people are thrust into the midst of significant managerial maneuverings, a viewpoint from which much tactical understanding can be gleaned. Many times one is directly subjected to interesting tactics from which a great deal can be learned.

Second, learning tactics requires that one accurately perceive tactics in action, a requirement that blocks the tactical development of most people because they are simply oblivious of the tactics being used on them. It is a wise person who really understands what's happening to him.

Third, the individual needs sufficient insight into human nature to enable him to sweep aside the facades erected by managers to disguise their real tactics.

A few words are needed in this regard because the average person is badly misled by the words uttered by the tactician. Perhaps nowhere is this so evident as in Washington, where astute observers of our administrative and legislative processes have learned to believe little of what is publicly said by our officials. Most statements are politically inspired or slanted and thus do violence to the truth. Overt actions are the key. What the people actually do is the primary factor to ascertain, not what they say. Indeed, cynics claim that some people automatically say just the opposite of what they do—the crook, for example, who loudly proclaims his honesty. One leading administrator, who had best remain unidentified, shouts to all how much he believes in participative management, but his people have yet to make a decision that was not what the boss wanted.

Unfortunately it is difficult to find much written about managerial tactics, and the reason is rather apparent. People do not like to speak or think of tactics, because it is not acceptable in our society to appear as if one is manipulating people—and most tactics focus on manipulating people or structuring situations. Moreover, many tactics, when improperly applied, are considered unethical by many people. In fact, there are probably administrators who would be more willing to talk about their private lives than they would be to talk about the tactics they use in reaching their goals, and for good reason. It is usually best that other people remain unaware of the tactics being used on them.

This leaves the learning of administrative tactics up to the individual. He must learn about them on his own. This is one reason that the development of managers is a relatively slow affair.

Perhaps it is just loyalty to my medium, but it is my opinion that a basic awareness of tactics can be had by reading. Bear in mind that one of the greatest and oldest (1530 A.D.) classics of Western literature, Machiavelli's *The Prince*, is about managerial tactics. The book would not have been read by so many generations in so many languages if it were not worthwhile. While there are many contemporary books about management and administrative behavior, most of which contain tactical insights, there is another type of book that contains a wealth of tactical material. Autobiographies and biographies of famous people can be tactical gold mines. The autobiographies of Ulysses S. Grant, Bernard Baruch, Curtis LeMay, Alfred Sloan, and Winston Churchill are but a few of such works.

There is another type of book, the business exposé, from which much can be learned. *The Decline and Fall of the Saturday Evening Post* is an incredible catalog of tactical blundering that should be useful reading for the ambitious manager.

Finally there is the trade press. With surprising frequency articles delve into tactical matters, such as was done in the November 1972 issue of *Psychology Today*, when one of the top administrators at the State University of New York at Buffalo gave his analysis of where his administration erred in trying to institute some rather significant changes in the university's academic affairs. It is an article on tactical blunders.

One can thus see that there is no shortage of materials from which to learn about tactical behavior.

Proper Use of Tactics

Tactics themselves are amoral. They are neither good nor bad. They are simply behavior, human behavior.

Whether or not a given tactic is correct or not in a situation depends upon many factors. There are no perfect tactics and in a given situation there is no one best tactic which can be used. Many tactics may work, some better than others; many others may fail, some more surely than others.

The tactics one selects should depend upon his own personality, the personalities of the other people involved in the action, the importance of the situation, the urgency of the matter, the relationships of the parties involved and their relative powers, and other unclassifiable random factors that always exist in managerial situations. This mixture of a manager's personality with the environment and the personalities of the other parties provides the challenge in the selection of tactics. The manager must correctly size up a situation to tailor his tactics to fit it.

All too many administrators mistakenly use the same tactics repeatedly, regardless of the circumstances. Such habits develop because those favored tactics have worked for them previously. Success reinforces the habit of using a tactic. But success can be addicting, much like the quarterback who develops a habit of throwing to a certain receiver in critical situations. There comes a time when it won't work, and that time is usually a most critical one. The adept manager has command of a wide variety of tactics.

The classic tragedy of managerial inability to vary tactics is seen in the case of the forceful, hard-hitting executive who, through the use of strong, authoritarian tactics, successfully climbs through the ranks, only to discover that at the top such tactics are not usually effective in dealing with others of equal ability or inclination. New tactics are needed for his new environment. However, he may be unable to make the necessary tactical adjustments, thereby bringing about his own downfall.

Tactics are the tools of the manager, tools he uses to effect his plans, get his way. They are much like a hammer that can be used either to pound nails or to smash thumbs. In themselves, the tools are neither good nor bad; one simply has to learn how to use them properly if he is to build houses rather than smash thumbs.

Terminology of Presentation

For the sake of clearly identifying the parties in a tactical situation, the terms "manager, administrator, executive," or "you" will be used to designate the initiating party—that is, the one who is faced with selecting which tactics to use in a given situation. Opponents are referred to as "adversaries" even though they usually are not truly adversaries in the usual sense of the word; they are not necessarily enemies. But they are the targets of the tactical undertaking and so are adversaries in one sense. This has its unfortunate connotative consequences, for it gives the impression that the manager is constantly battling with enemies who are trying to do him in. Don't be disturbed by the emotional content of the terminology. Most tactics are executed in friendly circumstances on adversaries who are unaware of being targets.

For the sake of organization, the discussion of tactics has been classified into four categories: (1) operating tactics, (2) tactics involving personal relationships, (3) timing tactics, and (4) negotiating and persuasive tactics. Admittedly some of the tactics could be placed in more than one category, but that is a minor matter. Don't let it bother you.

A Final Word on Keeping Your Perspective

Because of the encyclopedic nature of this book, one is apt to fall into the trap of assuming that the manager spends all his time selecting weapons from his arsenal of tactics. Nothing could be further from the truth. Such a scheming manager would be a most miserable creature, not long for his job. In the vast majority of actions, the able administrator uses the honest and straightforward tactic; he deals with his people and adversaries honestly and says what he means. But even so, a slight problem arises. How honest and how straightforward should he be? Yes, there are degrees of honesty. It would be a most clumsy manager who insisted on being totally "honest" (at least what he considers to be honest) in his dealings. Few managers can be completely honest with people without making many enemies. Moreover, there are situations in which using anything resembling this tactic may do substantial harm. It is in such circumstances that he must be ready to use other, more suitable and effective tactics.

However, the administrator wants to *appear* to be honest and straightforward in most of his dealings, regardless of what game he is really playing. To appear to act otherwise puts other people on their guard, thus inserting an unnecessary barrier into a situation.

Please do not be disturbed by the inclusion in this work of some simple tactics of which you have long been well aware. Such common tactics have been included for the sake of completeness.

2

Operating Tactics

Operating tactics comprise the bulk of the day-to-day tactics a manager uses in executing his daily role. In military terms, these would be called battle tactics. Keep in mind that the basic operating tactic employed by most good managers in daily encounters is the *honest and straightforward* tactic in which he tells the others the truth in a straightforward way. He says what he thinks. No cunning ploys. No devious evasions. All is open and above board.

Of course, there are dangers in using this tactic, as is related by one college graduate who complained to his former "Human Relations" professor, "You told us to go forth and be honest and straightforward. I went forth and was honest and straightforward. I got killed. Slaughtered! I was considered a naive oaf unworthy of further advancement. You left something out of your lessons. You forgot to tell me about all those people who are not honest and who are not straightforward." Let us not go into the fray unprepared, unarmed for what we most certainly will encounter.

The Choice of Tactics—Which Road to Travel

There are different avenues of approach in instituting a plan of action; the manager can select any one or a combination of several approaches or roads to follow. The wise administrator gives considerable thought to *which road to travel*, for inevitably they vary in difficulty and destination. Naturally, the manager seeks the path of least resistance; to do so he must evaluate the acceptability of his plan to various people. How much assistance and support can he pick up along each route?

A merchant constructing a store in a large regional shopping mall was shocked when he learned of the specifications developed by the mechanical engineer who had been designated by the center's management for his store area and for whom he was expected to pay. They had grossly overspecified 22 tons of air conditioning and far more heating capacity than was needed—cost, $14,000.

The merchant had several avenues open to him. He could protest to the shopping center's management. He could protest directly to the mechanical engineer. He could take the matter up with the proposed subcontractor who wanted the store's electrical as well as mechanical contract which were to be let by the merchant.

The merchant concluded that it would be hopeless to take issue with the mechanical engineer, because the man's professional ego was involved with the design and he would not be likely to amend his recommendations if challenged. He had developed these excessive specifications because his client's money wasn't being spent and he would be professionally safe with such an over-designed heating and air-conditioning system. Similarly, the merchant decided that it would do little good to take the matter up with the management of the shopping center for it was in their interest that such a heating and air-conditioning system be installed; they would support the mechanical engineer who designed it. But the contractor who wanted the job was a different matter. The proposed mechanical and electrical subcontractor was a large firm that had a great deal of influence with the technical management of the shopping center.

The merchant approached the owner of the contracting firm with independent estimates that only five tons of air-conditioning capacity were needed and practically no heating. The subcontractor said that he would handle the matter with the shopping center management. The final system cost $8,000.

This is an example of an assessment of which road to follow in executing a plan of action. Frequently success or failure in achieving a result depends more on how one goes about reaching a goal than on the nature of the goal itself. The manager must find a plan by which he can pick up enough bargaining power to have his own way. In this case, the subcontractor had sufficient influence and power with the key decisionmaker that he could carry the day. The merchant in the above instance did have some direct bargaining power, if it had come down to an outright battle, because there was nothing in his lease that required him to air condition his store at all. He could have sucked enough cool air from the air-conditioned mall to cool his premises. However, this was an ultimate tactic that did not have to be used, since the parties involved tacitly understood this without having it pointed out to them.

Sometimes the road to follow can be very roùndabout and devious; the direct route may not be the best. A person wants a job with a certain company. To apply directly to that company might be a mistake in many instances. Success might be more likely if the applicant has a friend place his or her name in the pot for the position. Indeed, many situations occur where one can go about achieving his goals only by indirect means.

Bear in mind, however, that the direct route is usually easier and quicker—virtues not easily ignored.

Never, But Never, Wound a King

Jerry Della Femina made mention of this bit of tactical wisdom in the foreword, but it is too important to let go at just that. In earlier times kings were not renowned for their kind treatment of those who attacked them unsuccessfully. The price of failure was frightfully high and rather final. The moral of the story was clearly that the party or parties who sought the king's life had better be certain of the results. Moreover, classic wisdom dictated making certain the king's entire family was also removed from the scene lest revenge be sought for the king's demise.

Well, kings now take many forms. They do not all wear crowns and sit on thrones. And there are many ways of wounding them. Let us restate this tactic for the modern manager.

Do not hurt someone who is in a position to exact revenge. If the injured party has a means to redress his injury, the chances are that it will be used.

Recall the college president who lost his job when he tried to usurp some of the power of the trustees who were directly, and closely, controlling his activities. When he tried to rid himself of the trustees, he failed—and paid the price for wounding the kings.

The attempted assassination of Hitler by some of his generals was dealt with rather severely. Their mistake was that they failed.

The futile attempt to unseat Castro with the now infamous Bay of Pigs fiasco resulted in his taking many harsh retaliatory measures.

The list of such failures could go on for some time but the lesson seems clear. If you're out for big game, be certain you have the fire power to bring it down. Hunting lions with BB guns is foolhardy and often fatal.

Law enforcement officers, the Justice Department, and the Internal Revenue Service all rely heavily upon information supplied by people who have in some way been "wounded" and who seek revenge by calling in the law.

Thus, the adept manager appraises the retaliatory capabilities of an individual or firm before selecting which tactics he intends to use. Definitely kings warrent different tactics than peasants.

The Fait Accompli—The Accomplished Fact

The *fait accompli* is an age-old tactic in which the person simply proceeds to do whatever it is that he wants to do. He thereby presents his adversary with the accomplished fact instead of risking the chance of having the plan disapproved. If a person is able to execute it successfully, the tactic is most effective, because there is usually little argument with success, no matter if the action was outside of policy or somewhat irregular.

Be warned that the tactic does have its dangers. Some superiors dislike brash subordinates who seize the reins to proceed with some unauthorized venture, particularly if it is a significant affair. This tactic is the stuff from which disciplinary actions are made.

But the tactic can be most effective in dealing with people who are lethargic, indecisive, or overly conservative. Knowing the problems that await him if he should request permission to do something or other, the strong manager may decide to go ahead with it and rely on his results and overall strength in the organization to protect him. Indifference frequently allows the fait accompli to go unchallenged if not unnoticed. People with little or no feelings about the matter just don't take the trouble to counter the action.

If the person is called to explain his actions, he can frequently cover himself by playing innocent. "Gee, I didn't realize that this was something you wanted to be bothered with, boss. I'm sorry! Thought I had authority to go ahead with it, that it was the thing to do." Flash a look of innocence and there is little the boss can do about it, particularly if the result was successful. The boss who becomes upset with subordinates who successfully execute a plan without his approval is apt to appear to others as a weak, insecure manager who lacks control of his operation—and he doesn't want that image.

This tactic works best in relatively minor matters. Don't ask your in-laws where they want to eat; they'll never agree with you and you'll be driving down the road for hours. Just pull in where you want to eat and present them with a fait accompli. Bosses favor subordinates who know when and how to use the tactic on matters they consider too trivial for their attention—"Don't bother me with it! Do it!"

Dangers are posed on more major matters, but that's where the real rewards reside. Jobs are placed on the line as some executives gamble their future on the outcome of a bold play. But then it may not be such a gamble at that if they are not particularly interested in their jobs if they are not allowed their play.

One newly hired sales manager, after interviewing each of his twenty-two salesmen, decided that fourteen of them had to go—there was no way they could ever work for him. Although the company verged on bankruptcy, he had accepted the job because he thought he saw a way to save the day while making himself some real money. He knew that his boss would be most reluctant to fire fourteen men at once—it would scare him to death. So the fait accompli. He fired the fourteen men, replaced them immediately with his kind of people, and had results to show for the action before the boss could react. He had little to lose. If he couldn't flush the deadwood, he didn't want the job, as success was most doubtful. And a sales manager might reasonably expect that it was within his scope of authority to hire and fire his men.

Corporate presidents are fond of the fait accompli in their dealings with directors. Time and again boards are presented with accomplished deeds for ratification—contracts already signed, financing arrangements already made, officers already hired. Sometimes token discussion is held on the matter for appearances, but usually the administration's will is ratified. Not always, however.

One Mr. Gilbert, former president of Bruce Company, undertook to take over Cellotex in order to merge it with Bruce Company. He went deeply into debt buying up Cellotex stock in 1962. Yes, the stock fell out of bed in the crash. Yes, he had a margin call from his broker asking for money that he did not have. No, his board of directors would not approve using corporate funds to bail out Mr. Gilbert. He fled to Brazil (unwisely, it might be added). All of this was a tactical tragedy because other tactics might have saved his empire.

Reasonableness is the key defense for the fait accompli. Make the action seem to be a reasonable one, one within your authority, and act surprised if anyone should question your right to undertake the action. Most job descriptions are so vague that the accuser seldom has solid grounds on which to stand, so the fait accompli feeds on the organizational confusion over who has the right to do what to whom.

It would seem at the time of this writing that the Watergate fiasco was partly the result of some subordinate executing the fait accompli, but with disastrous results. One can only wonder about the thinking of the man, because he had little to gain personally from the tactic and much to lose. A bad play anytime. Someone wasn't thinking very clearly.

Sandbagging

The fine art of *sandbagging* has been developed in the games of golf and poker and can be applied equally to management. The sandbagger in a poker game is the player who checks a bet and then bumps the person who does bet, thereby increasing the size of the pot over what it probably would have been had he opened the bet himself. The sandbagger in golf is the hustler who has a much higher handicap than his skill warrants. He has learned the delicate art of caring for and feeding his handicap, thus deceiving his opponents about his talents and intentions.

The sandbagging manager is similarly deceptive. He has mastered the art of seeming harmless and without power, but in reality he carries far more authority and clout than one would be led to believe. Sometimes his power is sub rosa, not easily detected except by those who have observed the scene for some period of time. Other managers sandbag by their seemingly pleasant, disarming personalities. They seem friendly and harmless, but in reality they are anything but.

The sandbagging manager sometimes will apparently go along with some plan of action, but secretly he is against it. He does this merely to lull the adversary into a sense of security and well-being. The manager has every intention of sandbagging the plan in some manner or another at a later date. Sometimes the manager actually gives his consent to some plan proposed by an adversary with the full intention of sandbagging it in some way later.

This tactic is used when, for reasons of organizational politics, it would not be wise to openly oppose the plan.

A rather unassuming department head disapproved of a program proposed by one of his men, but he felt that he could not openly veto it for fear that it would not only solidify opposition to his leadership but would look bad to his superior. So he seemingly encouraged the subordinate in his endeavor but killed the program at budget time by failing to find funds for it. "Sorry, Charley! Just couldn't get the money for you." And the sandbag claimed another victim.

Perhaps the height of tactical finesse was achieved by the chief of police of a large city who executed a double sandbagging. Bear in mind that the existence of a rigid civil service code makes the following tactical maneuvering necessary. Direct action such as firing is exceedingly difficult.

The chief was unhappy about the performance of one of his commanders. The vice and drug squads over which the commander ruled had been causing the department considerable embarrassment because of various incidents which had been widely publicized in the press. Let us say that there had been many irregularities in the operation of those squads.

In turn the commander was unhappy about the performance of one of his officers and wanted to get rid of him. This officer was involved in a drug buy from a federal informant and testified to that fact in court. Later the officer planned to soften his testimony, change his story, when testifying before another court on charges arising from the same incident. It was intimated that he was doing so to curry favor with the federal authorities from whom he was seeking a job. The commander was aware of the officer's plan to perjure himself and planned to let him do so, then sandbag him with perjury charges before the police disciplinary board, a charge that would lead to dismissal.

The chief learned of the commander's plan to sandbag the officer and sandbagged the commander after the matter had sufficiently developed. The commander resigned without comment.

Ray and Harry were fellow salesmen working out of a midwestern branch office of a large paper company. Expense-account policy was a frequent topic of conversation between the two men. Over the years, Harry led Ray to believe that he regularly included a few extremely questionable outlays in his "swindle sheet," whereas in fact Harry played it straight. Ray began inserting a few fudge factors in his expense reports. Nothing was said by the branch manager, so Ray continued. One day the branch manager was allowed by his superior to look for employment elsewhere. Harry was promoted to the managership over Ray in spite of Ray's superior capabilities. Reason: "Ray seems to be rather careless in his spending of corporate funds. We like men who know how to take care of our money." Ray had been sandbagged. Harry knew full well top management's attitude toward expenses.

Avoid Battle

In ancient times Hannibal threatened Rome from the north with his legions, which up to that time had rolled over a great deal of territory and several sizable armies. Rome's prospects were not bright. Most of Rome's leaders were all for going out to meet the Carthagenian cutthroat head-on in direct battle on the plains of northern Italy. This was precisely what Hannibal wanted, because his superior cavalry would then have sufficient room to maneuver. To that end he halted his advance in the northern plains to give the Roman legions an opportunity to come out to meet him.

However, he reasoned without taking Fabius into consideration. The Roman army was under the direction of Fabius, who correctly foresaw the folly of trying to defeat Hannibal in direct battle. Instead he developed a guerrilla type campaign against the Carthagenians. His army kept to the hills, avoided battle, and harassed Hannibal at every point. Unfortunately for Rome, Fabius' six-month appointment as general of the army expired and the hotheads in Rome who were eager for battle (but who did not have to fight that battle themselves) placed the army in charge of two men, each of whom commanded on alternate days (How in the world did the Romans ever amount to much with thinking like that?). One of the commanders had some reason about him, but the other was a rash, battle-eager muttonhead. On his day to command he marched his army out to meet Hannibal directly, under just the conditions that Hannibal had been hoping for. It was a massacre. Out of the 76,000 men Rome sent into battle, 70,000 stayed there, permanently.

The wise administrator *avoids battle* when it is not to his advantage to engage the enemy.

Choose Your Battleground

The actual scene or environment in which contact with an adversary takes place is not something which may be left to chance; rather, it should be considered very carefully. It may be wise to see some people in social environments rather than in the office. Frequently people are more relaxed and more congenial in a social setting, particularly under pleasant, relaxing circumstances, then they are in a business environment. Sometimes the manager should create the proper scene. In other words, the manager can *create his own battleground*, one that he feels will facilitate whatever plan he has in mind.

In a business context, consideration should be given to the question of where contacts should be made—his office, yours, or someone else's.

Sometimes a superior can gain advantages by intimidating subordinates through contact in the superior's office, but this is not always so. Sometimes subordinates can be impressed if the superior comes to their office, particularly if it looks like a casual visit. Sometimes executives have special rooms or comfortable lounges for creating a casual atmosphere in which to relax.

Sometimes an adversary can be placed in a situation in which he cannot oppose your plan because of the witnesses who are present.

Fundamentally, the selection of a battleground is determined by what influence the manager wants the atmosphere to have on the adversary. Does he want the environment to intimidate or influence the target, or does he want the environment to relax and lower the adversary's guard? A personnel manager for a large corporation was instituting a plan whose goal was to procure more and better college graduates for his firm. In particular, he wished to influence a certain professor to guide him to outstanding graduates. He wisely decided that his country club would be the best environment in which to gain the professor's cooperation. Armstrong Cork pursued a similar plan on a nationwide scale for several years. The company invited a large number of professors to various central locations for a one day program at the company's expense, and by so doing created a casual environment in which it could present its plan.

The chairman of one university department wanted his faculty to undertake a rather substantial, and somewhat innovative, revision of the curriculum, an undertaking that would entail considerable open debate. He decided that normal faculty meetings at school were not only too limited in time but also were not conducive to the type of discussion desired. So he instituted a series of meetings at his home in the evenings with proper debate-stimulating libations. The meetings were most successful.

The board of directors of a large lumber company had directed the marketing research department to evaluate the performance of one of the firm's new programs which had lost $4 million during the preceding year. The study found that the main reason for the program's failure was the incompetence of its administrative head. The company's policy was always to present research findings to the individuals involved for refutation before the study was finally submitted to top management. This presentation meeting promised to be a loud, bloody affair. The marketing-research director therefore rented a suite of rooms in a nearby hotel for the bloodletting so that none of the noise would be overheard by others. The battlefield was isolated from the other troops in order that their morale not be affected.

Be Present on the Battlefield

There are times when a manager executes a plan through subordinates, much as a general fights a war through his chain of command. Nevertheless, most good generals attempt to stay *close to the battlefield* for many reasons: communications are quicker and more accurate; more flexibility can be inserted into plans, should they need revision due to the course of events; and the presence of the manager on the battlefield can have a positive effect on one's forces and a negative effect on the opposition.

The manager should be present when one of his subordinates is presenting a plan that he particularly desires to be successful. He should lend his support and the authority of his position to his subordinate lest he expose the subordinate to counterattacks which may shoot down the plan in such a way that it would be difficult to revive later. Once a plan has been defeated, it will stiffen the backbone of the opposition. They can always claim that the matter has been settled previously and, therefore, should not be brought up again.

Naturally, there are instances when the manager should be absent from the battlefield. When he knows things are going to be brought up and said that he does not want to hear, he should vanish. Sometimes one's subordinates can say things that the manager cannot say or would not care to be on record as having said.

A more pressing engagement prevented a dean from attending a routine faculty meeting. Suddenly the dean's supporters had their hands full trying to table several outrageous motions put forth by the dean's adversaries, who had decided to take advantage of his absence to trim his authority. When the cat's away . . .

The matter of being at the office or in the store is pertinent here. One college manager had his operations so well organized that he really had little to do in his office. He only came to work when there was some meeting, and he would go home when there was no more work for him that day. Then he began to notice one subordinate was assuming some of his leadership responsibilities in his absence. He decided to spend more time on the battlefield so his troops could keep on rallying around his leadership.

A successful merchant began enjoying his prosperity by seeking the diversions offered by his country club. Every nice, warm afternoon would find him on the links. Then one day his accountant informed him that his success was in jeopardy. Sales were down, profits had evaporated. It's an old, oft-told tale—when the cat's away, not only will the mice play but also a few of the rats will steal. The merchant's handicap had to rise from seven to twelve before he turned the situation around.

No doubt former Attorney General Mitchell now wishes he had not been at a couple of battlefields in the Watergate caper. No executive of his stature should ever have listened to such a plan as was evidently outlined to him and a few others in his office by Mr. Liddy, even if he did reject it. The subordinate erred seriously in bringing Liddy to Mitchell's office for such a presentation, let alone having Mitchell listen to it in front of other people. Terrible tactics!

Recall the tales of the two deans who lost their jobs largely because they were not with their troops on the battlefield enough to establish rapport between the leaders and the led. These cases are prize examples of the need for one's personal presence where operations are underway. Most experts have decried for decades the evils of absentee ownership or absentee leadership. Yet there are those egotistical managers who think that they need not personally attend to affairs but instead that handpicked lackeys can tend to the store. Experience indicates otherwise. Numerous interviews with successful business people clearly show how close they stay to their organizations. Indeed, several outstanding administrators described the process of establishing their leadership over a new organization. They systematically try to meet with all, or the key, people in the organization to establish a personal bond, as well as to learn a great deal about each person and his attitudes toward organizational problems.

Perhaps you have heard of the classic industrialists of the old school who would walk each morning through the plant talking to the men and sizing up the operation. Those men knew what they were doing. They were visiting the troops before battle to let them know that there is someone "up there" who cares about them. Moreover, such inspections frequently disclosed problems on which action was needed. An experienced eye can tell many things at just a glance. Don't be shy about mixing with the troops.

The president of one large conglomerate has a policy of each year traveling from coast to coast by automobile alone and dropping in on various company operations unannounced. Many times he pretends he is a customer so that he can see how the company treats them. More importantly, he maintains, he is short circuiting the chain of command to get feedback. While many management purists would shudder at this practice, this leader believes that much information he needs for intelligent decisions was being filtered out by well-meaning, but protective and self-serving, middle management people. He insists that he discovers too many things contrary to what he is being told by his subordinates. He claims, "You've got to get out of the tower and into the field to see for yourself how things are running. When I walk into a branch and see a bunch of people sitting around doing little, I start asking questions about that branch's manager. When I find customers who are unhappy over our products or service, I find out why. Funny thing, since everyone knows I do this, I don't have to do it so often."

Make Certain Preparations Are Complete Before Battle

One should *go into battle fully armed*. Some managers are undone by their carelessness. Before battle they fail to make certain that they properly prepared, thus causing their own eventual undoing.

An executive was going before his board of directors to propose a marketing plan for a new product. His preparation was rather half-baked. There were several salient questions that he had left unanswered. After his formal presentation, several sharp-minded directors quickly made a shambles of his presentation with questions in areas he had slighted. He looked like a fool and his career was destroyed in that company. He resigned shortly after the incident, when advancement appeared improbable.

The editor of a large publishing house wanted to sign a famous historian to write a book for him. The historian had clearly stated previously that he did not want to do the book, but that did not deter the editor. He went to work. First, he talked with many of the historian's colleagues and friends seeking the key to persuading the man to write the book. After gaining some insights into the man's nature, the editor had a dummy book made up with the man's name on it in which the editor had printed all the reasons the historian should write the book. Then, armed with a signed contract and a check for an advance, he flew to see the historian, but only after sending the man's wife a small gift that one of her friends had indicated she cherished. The editor won the day. The historian was so impressed with the editor's thoroughness and drive that he agreed to do a book for him.

Touch All Bases

Frequently it is critical to attend to all the details involved in a situation. *Touch all bases* to insure that nothing is left unattended. Sometimes this means doing the paperwork, while at other times it means seeing all the people involved. One base left untouched may be the undoing of a plan. This is particularly true in attending to legal matters. The wise manager makes certain to touch all the legal bases concerning his operation, attending to all the little details such as proper minutes of stockholder and board meetings, and executing all the legal niceties that sometimes seem useless until trouble arises.

The president and majority stockholder of a corporation ran it as his own domain paying no attention to the legal aspects of running a corporation such as holding formal stockholder meetings, board meetings, keeping proper minutes, etc. He reasoned that he and the other two stockholders were so close that nothing would happen and there was no need for such nonsense. All was fine until two of them fell out with the third, at which time the third was able to use all of the untouched bases as trump cards in negotiating a settlement.

The vice-president of administrative affairs (the office manager) for a large insurance company had been reading a great deal about word-processing centers. After studying the matter for a few months, he decided that it held great promise for the company so he initiated the changeover after talking it over with the president. The wrath of middle management was not long in manifesting itself after their personal secretaries were transferred into the central typing pool. To say that the managers were very upset would be greatly understating their reaction. For a time the vice-president feared for his physical well-being. Chaos reigned in the executive suite until the secretaries were restored.

All the bases have got to be touched or you're tagged out. Consult with those people who are affected by your decision, particularly those in positions of power.

Personalize

People seem to like to associate best with others who seem personable. Cold fish are disdained. The manager who is always overly businesslike will seldom engender warm feelings. A great many things are done by subordinates for their superiors solely for personal reasons. The secretary who stays after hours to get out needed letters, the production workers who work extra time to get out a particular order, and many other such examples that happen daily are the result of personal feelings, personal relationships between worker and boss. Such relationships are difficult to establish at best. They are impossible unless the administrator has learned to *personalize* his approach to his people.

Take the matter of names. How can a worker think that his boss really recognizes him and his work if he continually refers to him as "You over there!"? Use names, first names when appropriate. Write little personal notes to people when the occasion warrants. Drop by their office to make the appropriate remarks when they have an addition to the family or other personal event which should not go unnoticed. One manager made a big thing of birthdays. He reasoned that this was the only ritualistic event that was truly personal with each individual, so he made certain that his subordinates' birthdays did not go unnoticed.

On a larger scale, significant business decisions can be influenced by personal appeals. The top executive of one small contract manufacturing concern operated on a personal basis in getting most of his business. By a well-formulated, thoughtful program of socializing and entertainment, he developed close relationships with most of the key personnel in the companies from which he wanted business. It is easy to turn down bids from men you don't know; but it is a far different matter when you know them well.

Sometimes a direct appeal for a personal favor will win the day when appeals to logic have failed. "I would appreciate it if you would do this as a favor to me." Implicit in this statement is that you will in turn do him a favor when the occasion arises, so don't be surprised to find the bill collector at your door at some future time.

Two vice-presidents who had been brought into a troubled company were comparing notes after a year of turmoil. The occasion was prompted by a meeting which had been called by the firm's president at which he had disclosed that he was having serious misgivings about continuing as president. He was under fire from the board of directors, who had lost confidence in him and his rather grandiose plans for leading the company to the pinnacle of success. One director referred to the president as a "megalomaniac," and said, "His credibility has been destroyed." The organization was upset and leaderless. One VP asked the other, "How often have you talked to him [the president]?"

The other VP replied, "Oh, I'd say we've said about a hundred words during the year."

"The same here," was the retort. "I don't know the guy and I haven't found anyone who does. He is a real loner."

The two men went on to discuss the whole affair and decided that the president would have to go. Moreover, they actually agreed which of them would take over the reins. And they made it happen.

Now what has this to do with personalization? A great deal. Had the president been able to relate on a more personal basis with his people they would not have plotted his removal. It is easy to do away with people whom you don't know, with whom you have no bond of affection.

Hold Your Coat

At times the manager wants no part of a battle. There are situations in which one is bound to be burned if he gets into the fray, so he should stay on the sidelines and watch the play, rather than acquiring bruises in it. However, the manager may have a stake one way or the other in the affair, so he uses the *hold your coat* tactic, in which he provides support to the warrior of his choice by doing everything possible short of going into battle with him. This is a particularly wise decision if one believes that the warrior may go down to defeat and one does not wish to go down with him.

Sometimes this tactic is used to encourage someone to do battle, knowing that he will be destroyed, to the ultimate advantage of the manager.

An executive with a large consumer goods company was rather controversial in his organization because of his aggressive personality. On one occasion he stormed into an associate's office with the notice of his annual wage increase, $1,000. He asked, "How much of a raise did you get?"

The associate truthfully replied, "Two thousand dollars." This added fuel to the man's fire; he threatened to do all sorts of things, including walking into the boss's office, slamming down the notice of the pay increase, and resigning. The associate commiserated with him and agreed that he had certainly been mistreated, that something should be done about the humiliation.

Actually, the associate had no objection at all to the man's resigning, for if the man did, the associate would gain certain advantages and additional strengths in the organization. So he executed the hold your coat tactic. The man did resign and the associate gained an additional raise for having to take over a few additional duties, which were no particular problem to him.

Sometimes this tactic is used to soften up adversaries. The manager encourages a number of other people to battle with the adversary prior to his engagement with him, in the hope that the adversary will be softened up by the continual onslaught and tire of fighting. In one company, a person did nothing to discourage four other associates from resigning for various reasons when they came to him to talk about their plights. He would offer no hope for them, thereby encouraging them to quit. After the four people had resigned within the month, he went in to quit too. He was able to extract most of what he wanted from his superior, who was now in a panic over what seemed to him to be a mass resignation of his entire group. It is indeed a wise manager who learns how to use others to fight his battles for him, or to soften up adversaries in anticipation of battles to come.

This is a relatively safe tactic to use, if done with discretion. The manager avoids the line of fire and need not take a strong position or say or do things to incur the wrath of the victors-to-be. It should almost always be used when one's allies are going up against very powerful adversaries—ones who are almost inevitably going to be the victors. There is little use in deliberately getting involved in a battle which is doomed from the start.

Frontal Attack

There are certainly times when the manager should walk right up to the adversary and make a *frontal attack*. This tactic is best used when the manager knows that he is completely right and that he is dealing from a position of overwhelming strength.

Under such circumstances there may be nothing to lose and quite a bit to gain by making a frontal attack that may even be quite obvious to all those around. There are instances in which if one does not make a frontal attack other people will be disappointed with him and lose confidence in his ability to make forthright decisions and act on them. One salesman clearly violated company policy by moonlighting on the side after he had been warned not to do so. His sales manager directly confronted him with the evidence and dismissed him on the spot when the moonlighting salesman admitted his errant behavior.

The frontal attack probably should be used by a good manager far more often than it is. After all, it is the cheapest and most direct route to a desired goal and, if it is handled correctly, the results should be quite satisfactory.

Unfortunately, some people have personalities which almost preclude the use of a frontal attack on them. They seem to automatically arch their backs and get ready for a fight anytime someone comes at them directly. There are obstinate, stubborn, contrary people. A frontal attack against such individuals not only is a waste of time but may actually warn and prepare them to defeat the plan.

The frontal attack is not advisable when one is in a weak position. If the manager is a voice in the wilderness, then he will have to use more guile to carry the day. The frontal attack will result in nothing but bruises to his ego.

There are different degrees of frontal attacks. Some can be most mild while others may border on violence. While the force of the attack will depend on the circumstances, one should lean toward caution, because unpredictable reactions may result from a forceful attack. People under heavy attack behave most erratically.

The tactics used by Roman Gabriel in his dealings with the Los Angeles Rams management seem pertinent to this point. When the Ram head office procured the services of John Hadl to act as "a backup quarterback" to Gabriel, who was publicly proclaimed by management as "the number one" quarterback, Mr. Gabriel said several unfortunate things in the newspaper not only about his feelings toward the new Ram management but also about his teammates. He was correctly quoted as saying that his teammates' selfishness was the reason for the poor Ram season of 1972. Such frontal attacks are bound to fail. No one can allow such forays to succeed; they will be counterattacked as forcefully as they were originally presented. Gabriel did not leave management anywhere to stand. Perhaps he did it with premeditation in the hopes of being dealt to Washington where he evidently wanted to go to be with his "friend" George Allen. George said the Ram's price for Gabriel was too high—it usually is for something you don't particularly care to buy. But that's another tale. Gabriel ended up with the Eagles. He was a victim of some shoddy thinking—his own. Had he played it cool, he could have had several more highly profitable seasons with the Rams. Hadl's presence on the team could have extended Gabriel's playing life significantly. Perhaps his ego would not allow it.

A noted expert on strategy and tactics, B. H. Liddell Hart, whose book *Strategy* carefully studies the strategies and tactics of the great leaders of Western civilization, concluded without reservation that frontal attacks are not only futile but a horrible waste of manpower. He maintained that without exception the great military and political leaders use deception and an indirect approach in defeating their adversaries. Seldom would the armies meet head on. The clever leader would rather by some device, outflank his opponents. Recall the measures Eisenhower took to make the Germans believe that he would attack in the Calais area rather than Normandy. He did not want to meet the German army head-on at the beach.

Moreover, Hart claimed that in personal endeavors the direct approach generates more opposition than necessary because of man's propensity to oppose anything new or any change. Since people are basically "aginners," the indirect approach is superior for many, if not most, people. They will be unaware of the play being used against them until it is too late to do much about it.

The Steam Roller—The Power Play

Sheer weight of numbers can carry the day against weaker opponents if one doesn't worry about the feelings of the other parties. Or, force of feelings may be a workable substitute for logic against those who hold their opinions lightly. A sufficiently strong show of feeling on your part may win out against a number of people not so highly motivated.

A branch operation was badly divided into two power groups —the in's and the out's, with the in's having control and numbers. Although for a while the in's tried to cooperate and work closely with the out's, not wanting to push the separation any further, it soon became apparent to all the in's that there was no placating the adversaries. Everything the in's were in favor of the out's were automatically against. They obstructed affairs in every conceivable manner. Finally the administrator resorted to the *power play*—we do it our way or you get out. He had the muscle to back it up. He only had to act once and the out's got the message.

While few people like to resort to the power play, still there comes a time when that is the only thing the adversary respects. If so, the manager who is reluctant to use his power will suffer.

There are times when it is a matter of who gets whom first. To tolerate the adversary only increases the administrator's risk. The general manager of a major league baseball team found himself with an inept team and a field manager incapable of doing much about it. The general manager dallied with weak tactics in dealing with some front-page antics of one of his superstars. The situation degenerated and the owner came in and cleaned all of them out.

Contrast that general manager's refusal to use his power with that of the general manager of the Baltimore Colts who, after his team's dismal showing early in the 1972 season, fired the coach and ordered the new coach to bench Johnny Unitas in favor of youthful Marty Domres. That's using power!

Perhaps time will tell if it was a wise use of power, perhaps not, for history does not always disclose the answers one seeks.

Outflank 'em!

The classic battlefield tactic for overcoming an adversary is to go around him—*out flank 'em*. This tactic is also highly useful in business. Instead of meeting an adversary head-on, the manager simply goes around him in some manner, thereby avoiding a fight.

A young man in a large corporation was having his career jeopardized by a superior who was holding him back. The young man outflanked the superior by requesting a transfer to another division for ostensibly good and valid reasons. After being transferred, he was able to continue his climb up the corporate ladder under more favorable superiors.

There are certain dangers involved in trying to outflank some particularly powerful adversary who doesn't care to be outflanked and who would move to block it. A direct confrontation may result. The manager must make certain that the person who is being outflanked will be unable to do anything about it.

Flanking can take many forms. Basically, it is the tactic of going around all sorts of barriers that bar you from doing what you want to do.

A dean would not give a department chairman money to pay for bringing a recruit for a visitation. The chairman invited the man to give a lecture, paid for from a fund under the chairman's control.

One high-income suburb had levied a rather steep tax on all businesses operating within its boundaries. Moreover, its zoning laws were used to further restrict economic activities among its residents. Numerous residents outflanked the intentions of the city fathers by using a post office box in the next suburb's post office as a front for the business they were operating from their homes.

The IRS prohibits individuals from deducting many items that are deductible for corporations, so the flanker forms a personal service corporation and avails himself of the goodies denied him otherwise. Most tax-avoidance schemes are nothing but flanking tactics.

Throw Your Own Party

An interesting associate once espoused and practiced a rather effective countertactic. If he was not invited to some party he felt that he should have been invited to, he would quickly throw one of his own and go out of his way to make his party more attractive than its competitor. Moreover, he would try to steal some of the key guests invited to the other affair. "If they don't want you at their party, throw one of your own!"

This tactic can work equally well in business, although admittedly it can appear to be rather petty at times. The president of a large downtown department store was snubbed rather badly and deliberately by the leadership of a certain charity drive. In retaliation he organized a nonprofit charitable foundation of his own to which he devoted his attention. While to many people this example probably seems silly—and I must confess that it fails to strike me favorably—still I will admit that there are times when it is important to a manager's position, his image with the people with whom he does business, that he not allow another person to "put him down." It is a matter of prestige and power. And these things are not to be taken lightly.

It would have been a more clever executive who found another way to *throw his own party*—one not so obviously done out of pique, because he risked being considered childish.

A seemingly sounder approach to situations in which one is shut out of some desired activity is to go about some other activity while totally ignoring the original affair. Don't so obviously covet the "party" from which you have been banned; make it appear as if you already had plans.

On a grander scale, a large group of influential business executives and professional people in one large city became so angry at the city's only prestigious country club, whose exclusionary policies were keeping them from participating in the country club life, that they threw their own party—they formed a country club that became just as prestigious.

One-On-One

Sometimes a manager endeavors to go *one-on-one* with adversaries; that is, he singles them out individually rather than facing them in groups. He wants a two-way dialogue with the other party with no one else involved.

The one-on-one tactic should be considered when you face a

situation in which there are several people involved in a matter and you feel that they may oppose what you want to do. You want a chance to persuade each individually without their reinforcing each other's opinions. People are more receptive to an idea if they are unaware of opposition to it than if they learn that other people also disagree with it. By using this tactic the manager attempts to block off the reinforcing actions of the opposition. This is particularly wise when the manager could be overwhelmed easily by the sheer weight of numbers, no matter how right he might be. He might be perfectly correct in wanting to do a certain thing, but if all his subordinates were to oppose him he might find it difficult to undertake the action.

Additionally, the one-on-one tactic allows the manager to vary his appeals and reasoning, to accommodate the particular prejudices of each adversary, a most important factor in effective persuasion. Some managers are particularly adept when dealing with one person but lose effectiveness when dealing with more than one at the same time. For those managers who are at their best in dealing person-to-person rather than with a group, the wisdom of using this tactic is obvious.

A newly-hired sales manager for a firm that was floundering on the verge of bankruptcy quickly perceived that some rather drastic changes had to be made in sales force management policies. Among his more controversial plans was changing of the company's method of paying its salesmen, who had been receiving compensation vastly disproportionate to their true value to the firm. While his superior suggested that all the salesmen be called to a meeting at which the new operating policies and compensation plan would be explained to them as a group, the sales manager chose to use the one-on-one tactic by visiting each salesman in his territory to sell him on the entire program, including accepting lower earnings in some cases. If he had called all 35 salesmen together to break the news to them, the meeting could have easily snowballed into a mass protest with each salesman becoming increasingly indignant at management. The meeting could have degenerated into chaos. By isolating each man—one-on-one—the manager had the opportunity to sell his program and give the reasons for changes. Not being exposed to the emotional stimuli which would have been forthcoming at a meeting, most men were rational about the proposed plan. The objections of the few men who aggressively opposed the plan were thereby contained and not allowed to excite the other men.

In another instance the tactic was used to sound out the opposition to a proposed organizational change. A young woman, who had assumed responsibility for supervising a secretarial pool of fifteen typists, saw a need for several changes in procedures to improve the work flow and relationships between the secretarial pool and the various executives using it. She developed a plan to remedy the observed defects. Although she was certain that there would be some opposition to her plan of action, she was uncertain from whom it would come. She used the one-on-one tactic to sound out each of the managers being served by the secretarial pool to see if he had any objections to her plan and, if so, what they were and how they could be met. After sounding out the executives, she discovered that her plan was acceptable with only a few minor revisions. She issued a memorandum which stated, "In accordance with my recent conversation with you regarding the work flow in the secretarial pool and the excellent suggestions you made, the following procedures will be . . . ."

The one-on-one tactic may backfire if the various people contacted are able to get together quickly to compare notes and discover that, as a group, they have strong feelings against the manager's plan. The tactic works best if the adversaries are physically situated so that it is difficult for them to get together, or if they are not likely to compare notes because of their positions or social groupings.

Unless the manager deliberately wants to play one person against the other, he should take great care not to give that appearance by telling different stories which, upon comparison, would quickly disclose his game. The manager's game may be destroyed once the opposition discovers he is playing one against another and they unite to put down his gambit. In the one-on-one tactic the manager is not trying to divide people at all. He wants them to remain an effective, operating, cooperative unit.

The development of effective one-on-one behavior is essential for anyone aspiring to a managerial position. The person who is unable to deal successfully in a face-to-face encounter with another person is severely hampered in his managerial pursuits, because that kind of encounter is largely what he must do day in and day out.

Muddling Through

The civilian director of research at a large military weapons developmental station was ordered by his superior to reduce his number of employees by 10 per cent (the famous RIF—reduction in force). It was left to him to decide who was to go and how—i.e., to select the tactics to be used in achieving the reduction. When asked how he went about it, he said, "I just muddled through. Didn't have anything in mind to start with. I thought about several policies. I could have gone on a straight seniority basis, but if I did I would have lost several of my best men as well as some poor ones. If I had unloaded my weakest men I would have had to dump some men close to retirement. So I did this and that. Natural attrition from turnover took care of a few, a few men retired, I fired some young men who weren't important, and I managed to get better jobs for some of the men whom I could replace. I managed to keep my key men. As I say, I just muddled through."

The tactic of *muddling through* is, in effect, to enter a situation with a mind to do whatever is expedient to solve the problem at hand. It is most applicable in situations in which the manager cannot determine beforehand what tactic or policy is most advisable in a situation, but rather must get into the fray and react to what comes up. He handles the problems as they arise.

There are dangers involved in muddling through. One can be inconsistent in his treatment of people. Moreovèr, he can give the appearance that he is uncertain of himself and not sure of how to handle the matter.

Its advantage is that the manager is able to get into a matter and decide what is the best thing to do in that particular circumstance. In theory, perhaps this tactic results in the most justice if the manager is able to execute good judgment on the spot. Unfortunately, when managers get embroiled in a situation they tend to become emotionally involved with it; and it is well established that emotions are a barrier to good judgment.

Divide and Conquer

Although dividing and conquering appears to be closely akin to the one-on-one tactic they are really two different tactics In the *divide and conquer* tactic the administrator may not be dealing with individuals one-on-one, but instead may be trying to divide two or more interest groups. Sometimes dividing and conquering will also use one-on-one tactics.

This tactic evolves in a situation in which the opposition is composed of several interest groups who have formed a coalition against a plan and have put aside their differences to organize against a common enemy.

In recent years the divide and conquer tactic has been the basic one used by Soviet Russia in opposing NATO. It has continually tried to insert wedges between each of the member nations of NATO, playing on their jealousies and special interests in prying them away from the common group, the NATO Alliance. We can see that in the field of politics dividing and conquering is a widely used tactic, but how about its use in business management?

Make no mistake, in some situations it can be a dangerous tactic to use, particularly when you must get along with the opposition on a continuing basis after the impending managerial action. The administrator employing divide and conquer tactics risks being considered Machiavellian, but this need not stay his hand, for there are certainly times when it is the correct tactic to employ.

To apply this tactic, keep each adversary aware of his differences with the other groups, and keep stressing that your interests and his have much more in common. Your major message is that it is more in his interest to ally himself with you than with the other adversaries; at least, you hope to neutralize him in the matter.

An executive vice-president of a manufacturing concern found himself in the unenviable position of administering a group of functional vice-presidents, each of whom was an aggressive empire builder in competition with the others. He managed to keep control of the operation through continual use of the divide and conquer tactic. He kept each of the vice-presidents loyal to him by not trying to solve their jealousies, but rather by using them to gain support. In many subtle ways he kept the men continually worried that their counterparts might get ahead of them in some respect or another. Each man was loyal because he thought that the executive vice-president was his best friend in the organization and that he benefited from this allegiance.

The divide and conquer tactic has even been used upward. One young assistant plant manager had a boss who was continually feuding with his peers. The boss routinely came into the assistant's office to let off steam about some injustice. The assistant took care to make the proper remarks, sympathizing with the superior's plight, adding whatever fuel she could, here and there, to keep the boss steamed up. The assistant had several ulterior motives. First, she wanted her boss's job and thought that if the man exploded in some company fight, she might get it. Second, since the boss had so many running fights within the organization, he needed the assistant for psychological support. This strengthened the assistant's position, so she received good pay raises and favorable treatment because her boss badly needed her.

The divide and conquer tactic can only be used when there is a real basis for the division. When the manager manufactures —or attempts to take advantage of—minor differences in order to split up the opposition, it may backfire on him and he will then face a united adversary whose backbone has been stiffened by the attempted use of this tactic. There is also a possibility that if the manager tries to use this tactic continually for small things, it will lead to his destruction.

If the manager does not have a continual relationship with his adversaries, he can rather openly use the divide and conquer tactic. Otherwise, he must use great finesse and subtlety in dividing potential adversaries, lest they become aware of what he is trying to do. It is quite possible to divide adversaries without their realizing it because of the strong emotions that are involved when someone harbors a grudge against another. Such emotions can be stimulated easily with little danger of discovery. Sometimes the adroit manager is able to apply the necessary dividing stimuli through third parties, thereby relieving himself of apparent blame.

In trying to breakup the oil cartel's grip on oil prices, the divide and conquer tactic offers the best opportunity. The OPEC nations have differing problems and do not all benefit equally from the cartel's policies. Particularly, each nation will be affected differently as the oil-consuming nations restrict oil usage. Moreover, each nation's need for funds is different. It is easy for a wealthy nation to voluntarily reduce its income, but it may be politically unfeasible for an improverished partner to do the same. Somehow we must persuade some of the OPEC members that it is not to their best long-run interests to pursue their present pricing policies.

Marshal Your Forces or Turn Out the Guard

Sometimes in a controversy the manager finds it necessary to marshal his forces in preparation for a confrontation with an adversary. He sees a need to overwhelm the adversary with sheer weight of numbers.

The cost of *marshaling one's forces* can be high, for the manager can only do so a limited number of times before his forces tire of the exercise. One university dean would marshal his entire faculty for critical faculty meetings in order to offset the power massed by the dean of another school, but his ability to turn out the vote at a series of these crucial faculty meetings waned with the passing of time.

The manager can only make an impassioned plea about the

critical nature of a meeting a limited number of times, so he should be quite careful to marshal the forces only in truly critical instances.

More frequently the manager moderates the tactic by only mustering a few troops for the confrontation. There are numerous instances when one is best advised not to meet an adversary alone. Perhaps fear for one's safety moves some managers to seek the help of others, but more frequently he either wants witnesses or wants to intimidate the adversary.

A personnel manager planned to fire one of the secretaries whose efforts in behalf of the enterprise were considerably less than what were expected. He had reason to believe that the young woman might react in an unpredictable manner, for she had a reputation for being not only somewhat emotional but also rather aggressive. Fear ruled his reason. He wanted witnesses —or help, if you prefer—so he had the girl's immediate supervisor and his assistant with him when the girl was told of her need for other employment. He hoped that the presence of the other people would not only help control the girl's emotions but that they might be useful witnesses should some unfortunate event occur. Such was his fear that he scheduled the meeting after working hours so that any commotion would not upset the other workers. Moreover, he had asked one security man to stand by without telling him the reason why. Ridiculous perhaps, but the man was cautious. He recognized that from such situations ruined careers are made and he wasn't interested in ruining his.

Aim at Strength

Some managers have successfully used the tactic of aiming at an adversary's strength, under the theory that when you defeat his strength his entire defense must collapse. Of course a manager using this tactic must be certain he can defeat the enemy's strength, lest he be defeated in turn.

One merchant, in selecting a location for his quality apparel shop, chose a site next to his leading competitor and set about to whip the adversary in the very lines in which his competitor was strongest. Through adroit merchandising he succeeded in luring away some of the adversary's best lines; in a period of eight years his business became four times as large as the competitor. Another apparel operator located in the same region attempted to compete by aiming at the dominant store's weaknesses, only to fail.

This tactic is best used in dealing with people whose talents are limited. A company was saddled with an obnoxious tax accountant of scant skill, yet the president would not approve of his dismissal despite continued pleas from the treasurer. Attacking the accountant's many weaknesses would do no good because all he was supposed to know was taxes, his alleged strength. He had to be beaten on taxes. His expertise had to be destroyed in the eyes of the boss and he had to be destroyed by someone outside of the organization, for the president would not be likely to forgive having his evaluation of the man shown to be in error. The tax accountant and the company's auditors had been arm-in-arm for years. They had a mutual nonaggression pact—don't throw rocks at my dog and I'll not kick your cat.

The treasurer decided that new outside auditors were needed. Some thoughts were planted discreetly among certain receptive directors by one of their own who was aware of the company's excessive tax bill and disturbed at the president's refusal to act on the problem.

And it all came to pass . . . in time. Indirect tactics can be time-consuming and many times they don't work. Things can go askew in the process.

Aiming at strength sounds so brave, so adventuresome. But it can also be stupid. One university with pretensions to being a big-time football power had a football coach who was fond of the tactic. The coaches were meeting one beautiful Sunday morning in late fall to plot strategy and tactics for the coming game Saturday against the nation's number one team. The coach announced a plan that was a cause of dismay to some of his assistant coaches. They would try to defeat Number One U. up the middle. Run right at them. Number One U. had an All-American middle guard on defense who was the terror of the league. No one could recall anyone ever running by him. The coach said, "If we whip Mr. All American's ass, we'll own them. We'll run all over them." While that might have been true, the likelihood of getting the job done was remote. Certainly this coach did not have anyone up front who was up to the task. The final score that next Saturday was frightful. Mr. All-American had his greatest day. Aiming at strength is not a good tactic in most instances.

In talking with the marketing manager of Hunt Foods I asked why the company did not promote its catsup more. The reply was, "Heinz owns that market. Why waste your bucks trying to fight them. We spend our money promoting markets where we can get a better return on our investment."

Aim at Weakness

A more common tactic is to *spot a weakness* in an adversary and take advantage of it: keep pounding at it, aim all actions at it, until the adversary falls. A football coach spots an opponent's weak defensive backfield man and that player will see footballs coming his way all afternoon. A weak defensive tackle can expect a large amount of traffic in his direction all afternoon. "Find the Achilles' heel and aim at it." People have their weaknesses and they have been destroyed by them. One manager destroyed a competing fellow executive by getting him drunk at the most inopportune time during an affair where key people were present.

Weaknesses can take forms other than habits. Sometimes an executive will have certain areas of his organization that are in trouble or that are weak performers. These are areas in which he is vulnerable to criticism. Executives have been known to be neutralized in their criticism of others by the existence of their own "glass houses." They cannot throw stones at another executive for fear that he will start stoning them.

Sometimes an adept manager is able to keep a discussion focused on areas in which an adversary is not expert. This is a favorite gambit of the quantitative person; he likes to talk in technical terms and stay in areas where the nonquantitative executive cannot even comprehend him, let alone counter him. It takes a brave person to counter this tactic, someone confident of his own judgment and prestige in a situation.

The sales manager for an automotive specialty manufacturer slowly became aware that the new, young salesman he had hired a year ago had become the boss's fair-haired boy. The sales manager's job seemed to be in jeopardy, but he was not a man to sit idly by while being threatened. He strongly suspected that the salesman's administrative abilities were faulty; his attention to paperwork and details left a good deal to be desired, but he was a great salesman.

So, the sales manager suggested to the boss that the new salesman be brought into the office as an assistant sales manager to give him "administrative experience." The boss eagerly agreed. The new assistant sales manager was quickly provided with much experience—paperwork, budgets, sales reports, sales correspondence, and expense account auditing. Not only was his work not very good, but he didn't do much of it. The situation quickly degenerated as the new man realized he hated office work. He asked for his territory back. The sales manager just smiled as the boss remarked, "I guess the kid fooled both of us!"

Run for Daylight

This tactic, named for the famed maneuver by fullback Jim Taylor of the Green Bay Packers, aptly describes a tactic of a manager who sees a hole or opportunity and pursues it with great vigor. This is a most desirable tactic. Dame Fortune smiles upon those who see opportunities and take advantage of them while the timid are left among the mass of the mediocre, too afraid to *run for daylight*.

There are few dangers involved in employing this tactic, except that one may fall on his face and fail to make it; but even so most people admire those who try.

A young, rising publishing executive, ensconced in a relatively high executive position with a large company, was offered an opportunity to head up the publishing division of a large conglomerate. The change involved considerable risk, for there was a high probability that he would fail, but he seized the opportunity and ran for daylight. Three years later the man was presented with an opportunity to go into business for himself. He seized it and is now running for his life toward daylight.

The problem with this tactic is that all too many middle-level managers really cannot see the holes and, when they do, they are afraid to run for daylight.

Speed

Plain, unadulterated *speed* is frequently a most successful tactic. History is replete with examples of battles won simply because one general was able to get somewhere faster than another. Business history is loaded with examples of firms that succeeded simply because they got to a market first. Executive action is no different. The president of a small manufacturing company was suddenly informed one morning by his two senior vice-presidents that they intended to oust him from the company by gaining control of the proxies at the next stockholder's meeting. They told him that they had come to the conclusion that the company no longer needed him. The president immediately climbed aboard an airplane and visited a sufficient number of major stockholders of the company to gain their proxies. There were two very surprised vice-presidents at the meeting when they were informed that they were out. Speed and personal contact carried the day.

An editor for a large publishing house heard via the grapevine that a certain highly desirable manuscript was being sought by three of his leading competitors, all of who were getting reviews of it. While they were dillydallying around with reviews, the editor hopped on an airplane and flew out to sign the author to a contract.

Some deals go to the person who beats his adversary by only a few minutes. Tomorrow may be too late in certain transactions. In this age of the jet and the telephone there is little excuse for an executive who sits back and waits for the U.S. Mail to firm up a critical deal for him.

The president of a small but extremely promising enterprise confided to a friend, "I often think that everything I have I owe to being ten minutes early."

The two men went on to discuss all of the deals they were able to sign because they moved fast on the matters. When there is something that needs doing, usually the quicker it gets done the better.

An old adage advises, "If you want something done, give it to a busy person to do." The truth of this platitude lies in the fact that really busy people have learned that they cannot delay doing a task; if they do, they will be inundated with undone work. They have learned that if they allow work to stack up on them they will not likely get out from under it. All their work will suffer and so will their careers.

"Do it now and do it quick" is the motto of most busy people.

Jump on the Bandwagon

Although the bandwagon tactic has long been associated with politics, it has other applications. One small group of students, desiring the signatures of a large majority of fellow students in a certain class on a petition, approached each class member individually. Thus they not only outnumbered each person in the confrontation, but also gave the appearance of a bandwagon rolling—*jump on the bandwagon,* sign the petition, it's the thing to do everybody's doing it. The more signatures that were on the petition the easier it became to get additional signatures. The power of suggestion worked well.

The laws of suggestion lead the adversary to believe that some plan is highly popular and that he had better join in support of it lest he be left out and thus made to appear to be a maverick. This tactic can be particularly effective against adversaries who do not hold attitudes firmly or who feel insecure and strongly desire to be members of the majority. This describes most people.

The manager usually endeavors to use the bandwagon to some extent in selling most of his plans. It does little good for the manager's adversaries to perceive that perhaps they are greater in number than they had thought. Frequently, this tactic is used in conjunction with the turn out the guard tactic. The presence of numbers gives the effect of the bandwagon.

In other instances the illusion of a bandwagon can be created by the sequence of contacts with people in the organization. A personnel manager wanted to change some of the paperwork that was required for various departments in requesting assistance from personnel in hiring new people. He knew his superiors resisted such changes as a matter of policy, so he did not try a direct approach. Rather he went around person-to-person (one-on-one) to persuade each of them of the advantages they would realize by implementing his proposals. Having gotten the organization's approval behind him, he went to his superiors with the message, "This is what all the department heads seem to want changed." He painted the scene to the superiors that the parade was rolling and that rejection would counter its direction.

The Trap Play

The thinking underlying the *trap play* is to fool the adversary into thinking he sees a weakness in your plan which he will pursue vigorously—sometimes basing his whole defense on it—only to be destroyed when you spring the trap.

One electronics firm, in negotiating cost changes amounting to about $500,000 with the U.S. Army, based its entire claim on an extremely lengthy theoretical presentation of what it should cost the company for all of the unwarranted work stoppages that had been caused by government representatives in violation of the contract. No mention in the presentation was made of actual, realized total costs on the contract. This was originally done because the actual costs were difficult to compute and could not be attributed specifically to any one work stoppage by the government representatives. However, any adversary would quickly see in the voluminous report, no matter how cleverly done it might have been, that the entire case was built upon theory, the theory of the learning curve and the effect of work stoppages on productivity.

The Army contracting officer quickly seized upon this weakness for his major counterattack, claiming that although this theory was good, the government was not going to pay off on theory. It needed cold, hard facts. He was trapped into making a statement that the government would pay on actual costs, not theory. When asked by the company representatives, "Then it is your contention that you would only be willing to pay the actual increase in costs?", the Army officer replied, "That is correct."

In anticipation of this counterattack, the electronics company's executives had held in reserve another report showing its total actual increase in costs, which significantly exceeded the theoretical totals it was claiming. The contracting officer was trapped. He had tentatively agreed to something in the belief that he had his adversary defeated, only to be demolished by his own argument.

Many times an adversary, when he thinks that he is successfully counterattacking and gaining a great deal of ground by pursuing one line of attack, gets carried away with himself and makes extreme statements or commitments based on that counterattack. Salesmen frequently use this tactic when they employ what is known as the "trap close." The prospect makes a strong objection to something or other. The salesman, knowing full well that he can meet that objection completely, gets the prospect to commit himself by saying that if his objection is answered he will definitely buy the product. Sometimes the salesman will even have the prospect sign a sales contract with the provision that the particular objection, perhaps price or delivery, must be met first. Once the person is on paper, it is difficult for him to back out.

An entrepreneur felt he was being badly damaged by a large company in violation of the Sherman Act. His lawyer confirmed the opinion. Instead of objecting immediately to the offending behavior with the possibility of having it discontinued or having it better covered up, the two launched a trap play. They continued relationships with the large concern while carefully gathering evidence. No longer were contacts made by telephone, a device which provides scant evidence that is usable. Now letters were exchanged. Witnesses were noted and, unknowing to them, were schooled in what was going on. The businessman just made certain that each witness saw what there was to see. One can not go to court without solid evidence, and to get it the trap play is a tactic that is widely used.

Harass

Sometimes managers who are in a position where they cannot win a clear-cut victory, may choose to *harass* the foe in such a manner that he will eventually give way. Such harassment can be quite subtle and almost invisible if the manager is sufficiently clever. Sometimes managers use this technique to force a person to resign. Frequently it is politically unwise to fire a person outright, but he can be harassed to the point where he will resign. His budgets can be trimmed, his best subordinates can be transferred out from under him, his privileges can be withdrawn, his authority can be reduced, he can be snubbed, bypassed, and soon he gets the message and moves on. Usually people have sufficient pride so that unfair treatment and continual lowering of status will cause them to go elsewhere.

One significant minority stockholder in a closed corporation was being frozen out by the majority stockholder. Since the law offered little assistance, the only tactic open to him was continual harassment through stockholder suits aimed at various malpractices of which management was guilty. Finally management concluded it was best to settle with him.

Of course harassing techniques may backfire if the adversary becomes angered and has sufficient power to counterattack or withstand the harassment. The psychological makeup of the adversary is most important in determining the eventual success of harassment. Some people simply cannot withstand a long period of harassment, whereas others seem to thrive on prolonged skirmishes.

One thing should be made clear to the person being harassed: what he must do to stop the harassment. This can cause a problem, for many times it is difficult to directly approach the adversary on the subject because the proposition sounds like blackmail. More subtle means are necessary for getting the message to the adversary.

It grieves me to report that this tactic is a favorite of some governmental agencies which, for fear of harassment, shall go unnamed. In the Senate Watergate hearings the Senators for some strange reason thought it most unethical for members of the administration to suggest to another government agency that it stop harassing Mr. Stans, former Secretary of Commerce. It did not seem to bother them one whit that the government admitted to harassing an individual, Mr. Stans.

Get Lost!

There comes a time when the opposite tactic to keeping close should be employed; that is, *get lost!* Sometimes it is highly advantageous if one cannot be contacted by certain people. One young man involved in a highly explosive battle for a top coaching position was advised to leave town and get lost until supporters had secured the head coaching position for him. Unfortunately, he did not take their advice and remained at home. An enterprising reporter got to him and the man felt compelled to answer a few questions with what he thought were the right answers. Unfortunately, these comments so angered the people in power that he immediately lost the job for which, ironically, he had been chosen only two hours before. Unquestionably, if the man had just been able to stay out of circulation until his appointment had been confirmed he would be a head coach today at a major university, but instead he is an assistant coach at another school.

Sometimes, no matter what a man says, it will be wrong; and to remain silent will anger still others. The truth is that under such circumstances one must not see anybody if he is to keep from making a mistake. Get lost and remain incommunicado.

This tactic is usually most advisable in highly explosive situations in which all parties need to cool off and the presence of the manager can do nothing but add fuel to the fire. President Johnson used this tactic quite well during the 1968 Democratic convention. His presence there would probably have done nothing but add to the chaos and confusion.

Getting lost can be an effective way of saying no without actually being forced to say it. On some timely matter on which a decision must be made, a wise manager who wishes to say no without saying it may, by getting lost, just let it pass by without saying a thing. This is closely akin to a presidential pocket veto. There are many ways of saying no without actually saying it.

Give 'em a Flat Tire to Run On

Ever try to go very far on a flat tire? It's rough! A newly-promoted executive vice-president of a medium-sized manufacturing company was sent back to the banks of the Charles River to become a more skilled manager, a more adroit businessman. Among other things he learned during his short stay in the hallowed halls of ivy while attending the Executive Development Program was that participative management was good. He learned about Theory X and Theory Y and that Y was good and X was bad. He was told he had marketing myopia and that innovation was to be the salvation of his economic soul. So he returned filled with much enthusiasm and a great sense of purpose.

His plant was ably managed by a man who had spent many long years with his nose to the grindstone, but no matter—Flat Nose would have to innovate and he would do so by allowing his people to participate. The plant needed a committee for innovation, it was decreed, and Flat Nose was to appoint it.

Now Flat Nose had spent a good deal of time getting his shop to operate just the way he wanted it to run and was not about to let this Charles River fever spread among his crew. He appointed the committee as ordered. He selected the two most outspoken young men in the organization and placed them in the company of three old mossbacks who would probably vote to rescind the development of the wheel if given the chance. *Flat tires* come in many forms but the end result is the same—the vehicle goes nowhere.

The manager can control what he wants done in an organization by the people he selects to do it. If he really wants something accomplished he must assign the work to a proven performer. If he wants to go through the motions for appearances, then he places the responsibility on someone in whom he has absolute confidence that nothing will happen.

Let Them Furnish Their Own Rope

Sometimes it is wise to allow the opposition to go ahead with its plans without opposing them, if one believes that they will fail. "Give them enough rope and let 'em hang themselves!" This tactic is particularly useful in situations where the actions proposed by the adversaries will not be particularly harmful to the manager. He can therefore allow them to proceed with little or no long-run harm to his position.

Sometimes he should take care that he not furnish the rope, for he must be able to say, "I told you so," by having gone on record in a most polite way against the proposed action.

The manager should be careful not to take a position in which he will be embarrassed if the opposition's plan is successful. He should not stick his neck out in opposition to them or visibly oppose or attempt to undermine their plans. His hands should be clean if and when the plan fails.

One ambitious young engineer for a large aircraft company had a boss who was addicted to golf. He would sneak out at every opportunity for a round, while the young man covered for him. The subordinate encouraged this behavior by being quite willing to do his superior's work. It was only a matter of time before the man's excessive absences were noted by top management and he was invited to draw his paycheck from another company. The subordinate got his job. As a matter of fact, this same young man used this tactic on three successive occasions to rise higher and higher in organizations until he is now a vice-president of a large aircraft company.

It was not golf in this instance that was the culprit, but rather the basic tactic of encouraging one's superior to be negligent in carrying out his corporate duties until discovered by top management. Sometimes subordinates have been known to speed up this discovery indirectly by arranging to have management's attention drawn to the situation.

A new general manager for a small insurance company inherited six department managers and four staff assistants when he took over the reins. After appraising his organization and its programs, he decided to make some changes in both personnel and organization. He chose four new staff assistants and wanted to hire a line assistant to coordinate the work of the six department heads and aid them in the development of some new programs. They objected. At a meeting called to discuss the matter, the department heads claimed that they would do all the work. The general manager backed off by deciding to *give them plenty of rope.* "Oh, let them do it! Then I'll either hang them when things don't get done or they will be so overworked that they'll be begging for that assistant."

The major limitations of using this tactic are time and damages. It usually takes time to let one's adversary hang himself and, in the meantime, the damages may be substantial. If the potential damages are minimal, this tactic can be most useful. More managers need to consider its virtues in preference to taking direct action against something of which they disapprove. Let the adversaries go ahead with their plans then use the results of their actions as you see fit. After all, the adversary could look rather pitiful if he were to say, "But you should not have let us done it." The wise manager may even go out of his way to go on record as opposing the plan but defer to its proponents for the sake of fairness, thus protecting himself.

Push 'em Off the Dock

Some managers practice the *push 'em off the dock* school of hard knocks in training their men. Give the new salesman a minimum of training, hand him an order book, point him toward the door, and shove hard. While experience indicates that this is not a good tactic to use in many instances, there still are times when it is the correct one to use. Good people may grow fastest when presented with a task for which they are not completely prepared and told to swim or drown. One thing about this tactic is that it separates the men from the boys.

The push 'em off the dock tactic is best used when the person is not apt to be destroyed by the experience. One professor used this tactic to teach his students the use of the library. He would give the class a long list of information that was to be located. Then he showed them where the library was located on campus and turned them loose. By the time they were through thrashing around trying to find what they needed, they had a good idea of what was in those musty stacks.

The key to using this tactic successfully lies in appraising the likelihood of the person's drowning. If he can do the job, then it can provide excellent developmental training for him. Unfortunately this tactic is used incorrectly in many instances. If a new person is given an assignment for which he has been inadequately prepared, failure is often apt to follow. Don't push 'em off the dock if they can't swim—that is, unless you want them to drown.

Use a Hatchet Man

When dirty work must be done, the wise manager tries to keep his hands clean. Perhaps he may have a subordinate, *a hatchet man*, to do his dirty work for him, thereby avoiding the dissatisfaction of those who do not approve of the actions. For this reason many managers prefer to have subordinates do their firing for them. Sometimes a board of directors deliberately brings in a president as a hatchet man to clean house and prune the corporate tree of its deadwood, thereby annoying the people in the organization. After all the bloodletting has taken place, the board can find other work for the hatchet man and a new person can be brought in who immediately bestows benefits upon a grateful, relieved organization.

One college president was undone because his hatchet man refused to do the dirty work. The president was therefore forced to bloody his own hands, thus incurring the wrath of the faculty and students. Normally, the dean of students is supposed to administer discipline, but this college president was unfortunate enough to have a dean who lacked the necessary backbone for the job. Instead, the dean referred the cases to the president's office. While the dean of men did not last long, neither did the president who had to handle the dean's messes.

There is always dirty work to be done in any organization, and any manager who believes otherwise is naive. There are people who need to be fired, budgets that need to be cut, bad news that needs to be given, and discipline to be administered. No one likes a person who administers discipline, regardless of how correct it may be. It is amazing to watch an organization come to the moral support of a member who has been fired, when only shortly before everyone was crying for his scalp because of his incompetence. The manager who fires people is apt to be a villain in the eyes of the organization. Thus many managers protect their images by having others do their dirty work.

The selection of the hatchet man can be a most interesting challenge. First, he must be willing to do the job, even relish doing it. Second, he must do the right job. No purpose is served if the hatchet man chops up the wrong people—and this is a big risk. Third, a good hatchet man, to be most effective, should come from the inside so that he can be well-acquainted with the problems and know where the bodies are buried. The outside axe wielder makes too many mistakes. But there are admittedly situations in which top management cares little about those mistakes, just so long as action is taken. They want people laid off and care little about who takes the fall. A wiser top management does not want to throw out the baby with the bath water. It wants the hatchet man to prune only the deadwood from the tree, not chop the whole damn thing down.

Finally, a good inside hatchet man must have some secure place into which he can retire safely after the bloodbath is over. Obviously, these job specifications make the position difficult to fill. However, there are some answers.

One university was in dire need of a president who would do some quick hatchet work on administrative overhead and some faculty members who were less than competent. Moreover, some of the university's programs were floundering and badly needed overhauling. Clearly, some leader with the guts to do the job quickly was needed. The board of regents saw this and appointed a tenured professor of recognized status within the university as acting president until a more permanent president could be persuaded to take the job. The professor had no interest in the job longer than a year or two. It was clearly understood between the man and the board that he would take all the actions that were called for to straighten out the mess left by the former president. When the ordeal was completed he would return to his tenured position on the faculty. He knew the things to do, had the motivation to do them, and had a safe place to hide when it was over. Though he admits that many of his peers no longer talk to him, he does not feel as if he is missing them much.

A person who is on the verge of retirement sometimes makes a suitable hatchet man. He can do his work and then retire. The classic answer has been the management consultant—bring in the consultant to do the dirty work and when it is over fire him.

Don't Burn Your Bridges Behind You

This age-old tactic is still as sound today as it was years ago. Generals and managers from time immemorial have made the mistake of *burning bridges behind them* that they later needed. This is probably the one mistake that is made more frequently in society today than any other. In the heat of anger, upon resignation or some other occurrence, an individual says or does things that permanently alienate others. He does this in the belief that these people will never be in a position in the future to affect his fortunes. Unfortunately, all too frequently these chickens come home to roost at some future time. He runs into one of the bridges he burned and is promptly stymied. One never knows what the future holds or who the people are with whom one will later come in contact. Some inconsequential clerk may someday be in a position to stymie the manager's plan. The salesman who alienates a receptionist may find that she is able to torpedo his sale to her boss.

The wise man goes even further—he goes out of his way to keep his bridges in good repair.

A young salesman of some skill became unhappy with the penurious policies of his employer, so he got a better job. During his last few weeks on the job he took what he considered to be just revenge by generously padding his expense account, not working very hard, and "losing" his sample case. While this bridge burning did him no harm on his new job, it came home to haunt him every time he tried to get another job, because his first employer would give him a bad recommendation.

And it works the other way, too. When firing people, some bosses so anger them that the victims do unfortunate things in revenge. The desire for revenge always lurks just beneath the surface, waiting to break out when good judgment falters—and emotion blocks good judgment. Revenge is one match that fires bridges. Snobbery is another.

While management trainees with a large company, Harry and Bill became good friends, as did their wives. The two families were quite close for two years and then Harry was promoted. He and his wife started traveling in new social circles. They dropped Bill and his wife, not an uncommon occurrence and in many cases one that may be necessary. But in this instance, Bill was soon promoted also and eventually rose to be Harry's boss. He never forgave Harry's earlier snobbery.

. . . Leave the Door Open

A manager should try to behave toward an adversary in such a way that the door is always left open for the two to get together on their differences. Care should be taken in what is said and done that the door is not permanently closed on communications between the two and relationships between them permanently severed. For this reason, ultimatums should be avoided, because they have a tendency to be final and to force an adversary to do things the manager might not appreciate. One keeps the door open by refraining from making remarks that are final, using instead such words as "perhaps," "maybe," "might," and avoiding definite finalizing exclamations such as, "under no circumstances . . . ." Also, actions such as firing an individual or resigning can definitely slam the door.

Admittedly there are situations in which one wants to slam the door because he wishes to push an adversary into action. Suppose a manager wished a subordinate would resign. He might clearly tell the person that under no circumstances would he be given a raise or promotion in the future. To *leave the door open* might provide the subordinate enough encouragement that he wouldn't resign as desired.

Events have a way of suddenly reversing situations. The old adage, "Treat your friends as if they may someday become your enemies and your enemies as if they may someday become your friends," contains great wisdom. Look at world alliances! To leave the door open refers to one's behavior toward enemies.

A new department chairman was brought in from another university to head up an average history department, over the objections of one of the department's senior professors. The new chairman was well aware of the professor's feelings toward him, but he made no mention of it nor did he do anything in retaliation.

To the contrary, he went out of his way to be cordial and professional in his contacts with the man, thus leaving the door open for the professor to come into the fold and join the team—he did!

Surrender Quickly

At times the matter at issue is of such insignificance to the manager that he is best advised, by quickly surrendering to his adversary's point of view, to allow his opponent to win the point. No fight, no contest. Few things will make a man quite so happy or disarm him for future conflicts so thoroughly as allowing him to win the day almost uncontested. You may wish to combine the *surrender* tactic with the capitalize on defeat tactic described in Part III to gain some ground in other areas, but that is up to you.

There is no sense in fighting every battle with every adversary. One must be careful to conserve his ammunition and energies for the battles that matter.

And another thing: when surrendering, do so with style and poise. Don't act like a loser or begrudge the man his victory. Be forthright! If the other man is right, tell him so. Nobody likes a poor loser, so smile even though you may be bleeding inside.

Perhaps you have known individuals who seem to have difficulty admitting they are wrong. They just will not surrender despite overwhelming evidence that they should. Such people destroy themselves rather quickly. Responsible people recognize such traits in subordinates and understand the dangers they pose to the organization. Most large losses in large enterprises result because the people in command are not able to admit at some point that they are wrong. Rather they try to go on with the error in the forlorn hope that something will bail them out of the mess. The people at Ford knew months in advance that the Edsel would bomb out but no one would or could do anything. No one could scream, "But the Emperor is naked!" There were millions of people who were trying to say the Vietnam War was a mistake, but the leaders would not surrender.

The shame of such matters is that the quicker one surrenders the easier it is. The longer one fights a losing battle the harder it is to quit. New product development managers testify that one of the most difficult decisions that management must make concerns the decision to remove a faulty new product from the market. After investing considerable money into a new product, it becomes increasingly difficult to jettison the project as the investment grows. There is always the hope that somehow the product will prove itself in the marketplace. Yet it is just sending good money after bad.

Run For Cover

There is a time for tactical retreat—*running for cover*—without surrendering. Sometimes the opposition is so strong and the situation so explosive that to start a battle would be disastrous, no matter how right the manager may be and how wrong the opposition. Other times you may not be ready for battle and should take cover until prepared. Philosophers have written about discretion being the better part of valor and that one should run away to live and fight another day. These are reflections of the run for cover tactic, which the wise manager will have use for sooner or later. The General Motors executive who had Ralph Nader tailed would have probably been wiser to run for cover when discovered than to have fought it out. The Shell Oil executive who murmured something in the Santa Bar-

bara oil fiasco should have run for cover instead. There are a great many explosive situations, particularly on the public scene where the press is involved, in which the wise executive will run for cover rather than make some utterances to defend his position. Remarks intended to be cute or to minimize the seriousness of a situation are frequently a grave tactical error which only serves to infuriate one's adversaries.

This does not mean that the manager needs to stay under cover, because many times he only needs to wait until the storm blows over. The tactic is particularly advantageous to use when a highly emotional adversary comes onto the scene who, because of his state of mind, cannot be reasoned with. If the manager cannot cope with the immediate situation because of such circumstances, then it is wise to run for cover until the storm is over. To try to oppose the emotional individual would only be throwing gasoline on the fire.

Other times one only needs to run for cover until he has either marshaled his forces or has obtained other support for his position.

A production manager was fond of playing the "statistics game" with his subordinates to "keep 'em on their toes." "Tell me, Gus, why did the absenteeism in your department rise 21 percent last week?", Or "Archie, your rejects were up 17 per cent. Why?"

The employees never knew where the attack would be launched nor what obscure performance statistic he would throw at them. Thus there was no way they could be prepared for the encounter, so they learned to run for cover. "I'll look into it right away, boss," and off they would run. Any attempt to give an off-hand explanation would usually be countered with more statistics, all selected to give the impression that perhaps the subordinate did not have a good grasp on his operation.

Clear Out

There comes a time to physically *clear out* of a situation—go on a vacation, leave town, quit the job, or take other action that physically removes you from an environment that poses great problems if you remain there.

A small businessman found himself in temporary financial difficulty that bordered on bankruptcy. He knew of some future events that were going to reverse his financial fortunes, but his creditors were becoming annoyingly persistent. Several threatened to go to court and throw the man into bankruptcy, an event that would have had a most unfortunate impact upon his future. The man wisely decided to make himself scarce until his money came in. A rather prolonged stay in Acapulco did the trick nicely. When his money became available, he came back and settled the matters. In the meanwhile, process servers were blocked from proceeding against him.

A young assistant professor came under vicious verbal attack by the head of his department one day in front of a group of students and fellow faculty members. The tongue lashing was not only most inappropriate, but undeserved. The assistant professor had every occasion and every reason to fight back and defend his position. He didn't; he simply folded up his books, kept his mouth shut, and walked out of the room. He said absolutely nothing. Under the circumstances, to clear out was a wise action—no good would come from confrontation at all. Everyone in the room knew that the attack was unjustified and knew the real reasons behind it. The man did not have to justify his actions to them and it would have been impossible to placate his superior. To clear out was the right tactic to use.

As a general rule, any time the manager finds his emotions

becoming unmanageable he must seriously consider the clear out tactic, because almost inevitably nothing good comes from emotional outbursts.

In a similar vein, one is usually best advised to clear out when physical violence is threatened. Three businessmen were on a "vacation" in the Caribbean. One of them had a problem with alcohol. One night he became overly saturated with the juice and began tormenting some of the island constabulary. One of the other men clearly saw it was time to clear out and stay away from the dispute. If trouble were to come, one of them had to be free to act.

Fold the Enterprise

There comes a time when the only intelligent tactic a manager can employ in a situation is to *fold the enterprise* He has no hope of victory and to stay and fight will only see him destroyed. It is indeed an intelligent person who knows when to fold his cards in a game. There are several advantages to this tactic. First, it conserves resources; there is no use wasting ammunition in a lost battle. Second, some unknown observers may be impressed by the wisdom of the manager who knows when to quit.

Sometimes it means resigning a position. Sometimes it means dropping a product, selling off a division, selling a losing company, selling a bad investment, or cancelling a plan of action. These things can be painfully difficult because of the manager's ego involvement. We just do not like to fold an enterprise. No one wants to be connected with an admitted failure. Rather, they would like to create a smoke screen to make the enterprise appear to be successful so that they can get if off their hands.

This tactic is close to the oft-given advice, "Never send good money after bad," which is one of the basic tenets of any good investor or businessperson. Folding is not surrendering. You don't give the adversary that satisfaction. Disguise your action in some manner. Brighter opportunities elsewhere can be used to explain one's abandonment of an enterprise, or the fickle whims of the market place can be blamed for folding the operation.

Be the Fall Guy

Sometimes the wise manager will deliberately *take the blame* for something, whether or not he is guilty, in order to ingratiate himself with a superior or to gain the gratitude of a guilty subordinate. It is a big person who admits guilt for something for which he is responsible. He who takes the blame for something for which he is innocent may be even bigger. It can gain allies and buy future favors.

This tactic should be used only in minor matters where the manager risks nothing by assuming the guilt. His action is only a symbol of his "greatness." The opportunity for such symbolic gestures arise often in the many little confusions and misunderstandings that arise during the normal course of the business day.

Your secretary makes a mistake in a letter. "I'm sorry, Jane. I must have given you the wrong spelling of his name." And who knows, perhaps you did.

Subvert

While the ethics of this tactic can certainly be questioned, it is still a tactic that some managers use. Its ethics can only be evaluated within the context of how it is used.

There are times when the manager finds it necessary to destroy his adversary from within. He may accomplish this by gaining the adversary's confidence and working from within to gain his way. At other times he may have spies or cohorts within the organization. Sometimes the manager pretends to defend the adversary in order to neutralize him and keep him from being forewarned of an impending action.

Sometimes this tactic actually involves espionage and the undermining of the adversary's operations in some manner. This tactic is an exceedingly dangerous one to use, for if the manager is discovered he may be destroyed. There is general contempt in the business world for the employment of subversion. Also, if the manager has allies in his subversion, he lays himself open for blackmail at a later time. Thereafter he is vulnerable to the allies' whims. It should take an extreme situation, almost a desperate one, before a manager resorts to *subversion*.

One chief executive in the women's apparel industry became practically paranoid about security measures within his organization after he discovered his phones were tapped, his secretary was dating a competitor, and one of his designers was unexplainably living far too high for what she was being paid. Subversion was quite real to him.

The inherent dangers of this tactic should be particularly obvious since the days of Watergate. Subversion is a tactic that offends our cultural values. Thus one who uses it opens himself up to serious criticism if he is discovered, even if he had the best of intentions in the affair and had every legal right to take the actions to protect his property. It is not a tactic that one can use safely.

Let Them Set Their Own Sentences

Frequently a subordinate has erred in his ways and, in a manner of speaking, is before you for sentencing. At times it may be wise to allow him to *set his own sentence* rather than your doing it. Some of the inevitable bitterness may be removed from the discipline if the man has established his own punishment. Sometimes you are placed in the advantageous position of being able to lighten a subordinate's self-imposed punishment if he has been too severe with himself. This can transform a somewhat sullen subordinate into a grateful one. Care should be taken to phrase your request for self-sentencing so that you are not automatically obligated to accept the subordinate's decision if you strongly disagree with the outcome.

A salesman was caught falsifying his call reports. As usual, company policy was somewhat vague as to what should be done in such matters, but it was understood that the manager could fire him if he so desired. But he did not desire to, because the man was a good producer. However, some discipline was required since the rest of the sales staff was watching to see what the rules of the game were to be, and the manager did want accurate reports from his men. He called the man into his office and presented him with his dilemma. "Jim, I value your services highly so I won't fire you, but I must not let this serious infraction of our policies go unnoticed. It may give the rest of the men the wrong idea. Think about it for a few days and then write me a memo on what you think I should do about it. Set your own punishment." By itself this tactic is punishment enough because it places a great burden on the man's shoulders.

A few days later the memo came. "Raise my sales quota $20,000 for the year and disqualify me from the present contest we are running."

Righteous Indignation

Occasionally there comes a time when the manager should display *righteous indignation* over some event. While the normal demeanor of the mature executive is usually that of the cool, calm, and collected intellect, sometimes such behavior fails to communicate precisely how one feels about something to someone who badly needs the message. The tactic can only be used when the manager is obviously totally in the right and the adversary has committed a wrong that cannot be allowed to go unnoticed.

The president of a small sporting goods manufacturing company had previously warned his personnel manager to stop being so friendly with the female employees, but the man's indiscretions continued. The president descended angrily upon the subordinate after hearing the complaint of a newly-hired young lady of considerable pulchritude, who objected to some of the demands that were being placed upon her by the personnel manager. The president summoned the errant Don Juan to his office and loudly and emphatically fired him after reading the riot act to him about his misconduct. It was not accidental that the president left the door to his office wide open during the performance.

Everyone in the office could hear the president's controlled rage. He wanted to make certain that not only did all other male employees in the company who might be harboring lecherous intentions receive the message loud and clear, but he also wished the women to be assured of his policy on such matters.

There is very little an adversary can really do in the face of righteous indignation that is based on incontestable facts. However, care must be taken that the adversary is fully deserving of the angry attack and that he has no acceptable defense, because if he does a real shouting match may ensue. Unjustified indignation will beget righteous indignation in return. And such is the stuff that starts fights.

Even so, many completely guilty individuals will fight back instinctively when so openly attacked. Silence would be an admission of guilt, so a protest must be made. Be warned that you can never be certain of the adversary's reaction at the time. You are taking a risk. You can be certain you've made an enemy of him, so be sure that he is in no position to do you any harm. The executive should take care that he not use this tactic often lest he garner a reputation for being unstable.

Silence—Maintain Confidence

This is a badly underused tactic, for most people seem to talk too much for their own good and fail to *maintain confidences* given them. It is a safe assumption that if you say something you do not want a particular person to hear, that information will almost automatically gravitate to that party. Indeed, one of the worst reputations one can develop is that of talking too much. Seldom is one criticized for saying too little.

Let us understand clearly the powerful force that makes people talk too much in spite of their knowing better. Usually they do know better, but for various reasons they simply are unable to control their tongues. First, talking is fun. It is social intercourse and man, being a highly social animal, is strongly predisposed toward making noises. The real art lies in being able to make noises without really saying much, while not having the other party perceive that he is being conversationally shortchanged.

Second, people who are insecure about their position frequently feel compelled to impress others of their importance and status by the spoken word. This, of course, is a tragic mistake. Seldom can anyone gain status and prestige through what he says. Status is usually achieved through one's deeds and what others say about you. However, the temptation to shorten the road to status is strong and people will continually undertake to impress others through conversation.

Third, many people feel a strong compulsion to make others think that they are on the inside, or are in-the-know. They talk in order to impress others with their smartness. It seldom works. Violations of this tactic are so numerous that illustrations are hardly needed.

One director of an electronics manufacturing concern was on a flight from Denver to Los Angeles when the man sitting next to him struck up a conversation. It developed that he was the sales manager for a competing company. That flight proved most rewarding for the director because he learned a great deal of useful information about what the competitor was doing that was put to good use by his concern later. The director never had to disclose his identity for he could hardly get a word in edgewise. It is truly amazing what one can learn just by listening to the talkers.

Knowing the dangers of excessive talking, knowledgeable top executives disdain subordinates who do not carefully control what they say. Careers have been ruined in one night of relaxation when the offending party was observed to be too talkative in social situations.

Lest you doubt the difficulty of controlling people's tongues just recall the unpluggable leaks that exist continually in the highest echelons of Washington. Experienced Washington correspondents say that they have no difficulty at all getting someone in the administration to talk. There is always someone who is ready to buy favor with his talk.

Take the Pitch

A well-recognized tactic in the baseball world is called *taking the pitch*. The batter, for one reason or another, decides beforehand to let the next pitch go by, no matter how tempting it might be to swing.

An analogous situation frequently arises in personal relationships. The adversary says something that presumably calls for a reply but it was not phrased as a direct question which should be answered out of courtesy. Consider taking the pitch—say nothing, give no reaction—so the other party will go on talking. This tactic is close kin to keeping silent, but with a different twist. Let's examine one incident.

An editor casually mentioned early in a meeting with the author certain terms for a contract that were not altogether unfavorable. He would have accepted them had nothing more been offered. However, no reaction was forthcoming and the conversation was steered in other directions. When the topic was resurrected later, for some odd reason the terms had improved.

The tactic is also useful for prying information from people. Many times if you react to a statement you will either cut off the flow of conversation or alter its direction in ways the other party would prefer. In any event, the whole truth may not be forthcoming. Take the pitch and let the person keep throwing.

Moreover, you gain some valuable time to think about what is being said and to plan your statements and tactics, if you will just let the other party go on uninterrupted.

There are times when something is very important to you but when you should disguise your interest in it. Take the pitch! Don't jump in with your eagerness because you may scare the other party or in some way lead him to behave in ways that you do not desire.

Act, Don't React

The president of a leading university developed the unfortunate reputation among his subordinates of being an extremely weak administrator, because he constantly *reacted to situations rather than acting on them.* Eventually he was forced to resign. He habitually waited until he was confronted with a situation caused by others. Then he would react to that situation in some random manner rather than formulating plans and programs before such situations developed so that they could be handled within the context of his policies.

The problem of always being in a position of reacting is that adversaries, once they learn of that propensity of the manager, will keep creating situations to which he must react. Amid all of these reactions, he finds himself giving way to the pressures of immediacy. In the long run his policies will be damaged. A weak administrator tends to try to get out of the immediate situation in the most expedient manner possible, but in so doing he creates situations which he will regret thereafter.

Many university presidents, in dealing with student groups, have shown their weaknesses in just such situations. Instead of developing firm, clear-cut policies with which to handle incidents as they arise, they have tended to deal with each student group as the situation arises, making policies and rules as the occasion demands.

It might seem to some people that a policy of reacting to a situation as it occurs would be a sound one for a manager to follow, since it should allow him to adapt his behavior to the particular problem confronting him. Yes, it would be nice if managerial situations worked that way, but they don't! There are some elements missing from the picture—emotion and adversary loophole-seeking.

In the expediency model, it is assumed that the manager evaluates all factors in the situation with cold rationality. But he doesn't. He can't! The manager's immediate involvement in a situation is always accompanied by emotion—often very strong emotion—and emotion blocks good judgment. It is almost impossible to exercise good judgment when one is emotionally involved in a situation. Since a policy is a premade decision, one that should be made with due thought and without pressure, one of its purposes is to relieve the manager of the burden of having to make a decision under pressure. This should improve the quality of his decisions. Moreover, when an administrator makes on-the-spot decisions during a confrontation there is great likelihood that he will create some loopholes, inconsistencies, or inequities of managerial behavior which his adversaries will immediately exploit. Thus another problem will be created for the manager to mess up. This can go on until the manager is so mired that he is in an untenable position, looking like the boob he is.

Immediate nonpolicy managerial reactions in serious conflicts are most dangerous undertakings.

Don't Act from Emotion

Continuing from the last tactic, an emotional mind is an unthinking one. Seldom does one make sound decisions when emotionally disturbed, because *emotions block out rational thought*. For this reason, the manager is strongly advised to never act in the heat of emotion. Instead, one should only act after cold, rational thought.

The president of a manufacturing company learned that one of his directors had taken it upon himself to perform certain operating functions in new product planning. The director had contacted some potential competitors to learn something of the business. The president felt this was unethical and reacted somewhat emotionally to it, thereby permanently alienating the director. The director felt the president's behavior was ridiculous.

The president of one closely-held mercantile concern became extremely angry with one of his associates and suddenly severed all relationships by activating a stock repurchase contract they had signed. This proved to be a most serious mistake, for the men were involved in a very complex legal entanglement concerning several of their investments which demanded complete loyalty and unity between them. Once the emotional merchant had kicked his associate out of bed, their interests were in direct opposition. In the end, the emotional outburst cost the merchant about $30,000 that he could have saved had he kept his temper with the associate until the affair was all over—and then parted company with him.

Test the Water

Sometimes the manager is wise if he tests the temperature of the organizational water before he introduces a plan. If the organization reacts adversely to his test, he may revise his intentions, but if it is receptive he proceeds to implement the plan.

This is a sound administrative tactic, because little is lost by trying it. The personnel manager of a large manufacturing plant entertained thoughts of staggering the working hours of all workers in order to relieve the traffic congestion in the area during the morning and evening rush hours. Before officially putting forth his idea, he quietly tested it both on the workers and on top management. He quickly encountered vigorous opposition, so he dropped the idea, thereby saving face. If he had proposed the plan without a test, he would have looked rather foolish when it was turned down.

A new dean of an engineering school developed a new organizational plan which, among other things, entailed bringing an outside man to head up all academic programs. He first tried his plan on his executive council. They didn't like it so he changed his plans.

Sometimes a manager who truly wants to disguise the source of an idea while *testing the water* may attribute the idea to-someone else, or to an unidentified party, thereby removing his own personal status from the idea should it be soundly defeated.

Laugh It Off

One devastatingly deceptive tactic that a manager can use to dismiss a criticism or complaint from an adversary is to *laugh it off* or to treat it as if he were joking and not being serious about his comment. Many times the adversary will quickly fold his tent by pretending that he really was kidding, whereas in fact he was not. This tactic is particularly appropriate when the adversary's criticism is so extreme that one would be justified in assuming that he was kidding. Laughter can be a devastating defensive weapon to use when one doesn't wish to discuss something seriously. One can laugh off a topic and then change the subject.

Laughing is a particularly good defense when one really has no answer to give. A bit of laughter combined with silence can leave an adversary completely perplexed and disarm him by your apparent unconcern about the matter.

A particularly aggressive door-to-door saleswoman was attempting a last ditch effort to sell a set of encyclopedias after an evening of failing to convince a particularly tough prospect. As she was departing, she made her last ditch close by saying, "Well, I'm most disappointed this evening. I came here expecting to meet a highly intelligent individual, someone interested in the welfare and education of his children. I see I was wrong!"

The worldly wise prospect just laughed and asked, "How many times does that last ditch effort work for you?"

She chuckled, "Oh, about one time in ten it gets me back in the door."

A holder of a businessman's note had legally exercised its acceleration clause to demand full payment when the maker was tardy with a payment. After paying off the note, the businessman was furious at his former creditor and ordered him never to set foot in his place of business again. The ex-creditor left, doubled over with laughter. This greatly distressed his adversary, who was left standing in the middle of his store shaking his fists in a rage over being laughed at.

A personnel agent was deliberately needling an applicant for an executive job to see how well he took the stress. He needled, "What's the matter? Don't you believe in shining your shoes?" upon noticing that the applicant's shoes were not polished.

The applicant laughed and replied, "I guess I'd better get my wife trained better, hadn't I?"

This neatly parried the personnel manager's thrust and showed that the man had poise. Laughter eases tensions and allows a person time to think of replies. It can sometimes ease the tension in a sticky situation, much to the advantage of all. It is indeed an exceptional manager who can see enough humor in a situation to laugh at it.

Laughing at the wrong time or in the wrong place can label one either a fool or a buffoon, because there are times and places where laughter is certainly inappropriate and not appreciated by people attempting to solve a serious problem.

Ignore the Static

In implementing many plans the manager must learn to *ignore outside static* being given him by adversaries and push on to a successful culmination of the plan. He should not allow himself to be deterred by minor assaults on his flanks and various noises being made by adversaries. He must figuratively wear earmuffs and blinders so that all he can see are the goals he wishes to achieve and the plan of action by which he hopes to achieve them.

The president of a candy company that traditionally made high quality candies sold through wholesalers to various dealers decided that the future goal of his company should be to develop a large chain of company-owned retail stores through which it would sell its fine candies directly to the consumer. He was fought on every front by his board of directors, his subordinates, his bankers, and his family. No one agreed with him. But he was an extremely strong leader, so by sheer force of his personality (and ownership of the majority of the common stock of the company) he carried his plan of action through to a phenomenally successful conclusion. He was right and his critics were wrong. Of course if he had been wrong he would have looked like a pig-headed fool. It is a risky tactic.

Once an administrator has made up his mind to do something despite what anyone else says or does, then he must develop a mental shield which will help him ignore the static that will be coming his way.

This tactic is particularly useful in handling minor, petty, trivial irritations. A great manager does himself no service by stooping to answer petty criticisms. One of the best ways to put down such adversaries is simply to ignore them pointedly as if they were inconsequential. To some extent all managers must learn to wear earmuffs, for there is no shortage of unsolicited advice. You can hear anything you want to hear.

One young entrepreneur was in constant confusion. One friend would tell him one thing and another would say something else. He became afraid to act for fear of making a mistake, and he didn't know how to determine the validity of the advice being given him. He finally tuned out the outsiders when he realized that their advice was superficial and given without benefit of good knowledge of all the factors involved in the situation.

The experienced and mature executive eventually learns to trust his judgment over that of others, because he is the only person who is in a position to see and integrate all aspects of a situation. After all, your lawyer, your consultant, your subordinates, your wife, and your friends have only parts of the puzzle. They seldom see the whole picture. Moreover, they certainly do not have access to your value system. Do not be misled. Your values are critical factors in your decision making. Thus you frequently have good and valid reason to ignore the criticisms of others.

Die on the Vine

Students of political science have recognized this classic tactic in the guise of the presidential or gubernatorial "pocket vetoes". The chief executive officer is in this case able to have his way simply by doing nothing—letting a matter *die on the vine*. This can be a most effective tactic to use in many situations in which there is nothing that is really compelling the manager to act. Thus the passive tactic of allowing a matter to die on the vine frequently escapes detection, because what is not overt is seldom perceived by parties other than those with an intense interest in the matter.

Sometimes the manager must also use the stall tactic to give the issue time to die on the vine. He simply keeps stalling and stalling until the adversaries get the message and decide the matter isn't worth pursuing.

One executive was blessed with a most able secretary who had a weakness for the presentations of salesmen. It was an inept salesman who could not persuade her that she needed whatever it was that he was selling—a new typewriter, new desk, new filing cabinet, or whatever. The boss always knew when a salesman had been talking to her, because she would immediately come in with the plea that she needed this or that.

After granting a few of her requests, he soon perceived the game and altered his tactics. The conversation would go something like, "You know, Mr. Boss, I could really use a new desk."

"Oh, Marie, is that so?"

"Yes, I saw one just the other day that would really be nice."

"Well, write me a memo about it and I'll forward it to purchasing and we'll see what we can do."

Upon receipt of Marie's memo, the boss forwarded the memo to a knowing purchasing agent who pigeonholed it. Marie's desire for the desk waned when the next salesman gave her his pitch. She was just a person who couldn't say no.

Admittedly, many times this tactic won't work. The executive tries to let a matter die on the vine and the adversary won't have any part of it, but instead insists upon forcing the executive to take some action. However, seldom has much harm accrued to the manager in such instances, other than antagonizing the adversary somewhat and possibly projecting a do-nothing image to other people who know of the incident.

Let 'em Bitch

Some managers deliberately set up sessions at which their subordinates can *voice their feelings* concerning some plan of action. He does this not because he is going to change the plan one iota because of what is said, but just to allow the people to get the frustrations and feelings out of their systems.

The Denver school board was considering instituting a plan for busing students to achieve racial balance in the schools. Finally it made up its mind to go ahead with the program. But first it held an open meeting at which it promised that everyone who wanted to speak would be heard. The session lasted six hours—into the wee hours of the morning—and more than 150 people spoke for and against the plan. It was quite a spectacle and a good many people probably felt better afterwards for having vented their feelings. In the end, the board went ahead and voted for the plan that they were going to vote for in the first place.

A manager must be certain that he has absolute control over a situation and that such sessions will not get out of control and result in jeopardizing his position.

On a one-on-one basis, the wise manager frequently lets the other party complain to his heart's content. It can be good therapy. But take warning: care should be taken that the adversary not gain false ideas during such sessions. It is all too easy for the manager to nod his head or otherwise give some signal that might be falsely interpreted by the other party. It is all too easy for the adversary to interpret a manager's silence as consent or agreement when he is only exhibiting courtesy. The person should not leave the meeting with thoughts other than those intended by the manager.

The Hot Potato

Some issues are so potentially explosive that the wise manager avoids being connected with them. He passes *the hot potato* on to other people.

The My Lai massacre provides an excellent case in point. The incident evidently was covered up and passed along by a long line of officers, because they recognized it to be the hot potato it truly was. No one was about to pry the lid off that can of worms. Their tactic would have worked had not the whistle been blown on the affair by outsiders. Even after disclosure anyone with good judgment correctly sensed its career-busting potentialities and thus avoided contact with it as best they could.

Administrators in public positions must become quite adept at not allowing hot potatoes to be dumped into their laps because they will inevitably be burned, no matter how well they handle them. Pity the administrator—such as the Mayor of New York—who continually has hot potatoes of the greatest magnitude dumped into his lap day after day.

This tactic is closely akin to passing the buck. The difference is that sometimes the manager does not have to pass a hot potato on, but can merely avoid having it dumped into his lap when he realizes that now is not the time to become involved with that hot issue.

The wife of George, a department head, became disenchanted with one of her husband's secretaries ("She is rude to me!") and insisted the secretary had to go. George took his problem to the dean, who said he would try to arrange a swap. The dean approached Don, another department head, with the tale and asked if he would trade secretaries to help out his harassed colleague.

Now it so happened that Don had two secretaries, both of whom were quite happy in their positions, and his faculty members were quite happy with them. It had not always been so and Don had no desire whatsoever to disrupt his happy operation. He told the dean just that and asked, "How in hell did you get involved in this mess? As I see it, it's George's secretary, it's George's wife, and that makes it George's problem. How did you get sucked into it?"

"I don't know. Momentary lapse of judgment, I guess. You're right, it's not my problem. We'll just let George handle it," the dean replied.

Don't deal yourself cards in someone else's game.

Innocent All the Way

In the summer of 1971, as the specter of a disastrous season began shattering baseball careers, Tony Conigliaro quit the California Angels at the same time as his brother, Billy, was having some difficulty with his employers, the Boston Red Sox. In an unwise interview with newspapermen, Billy C. alleged that his brother, Tony, had been traded from the Red Sox to the Angels the previous year at the insistence of Carl Yastrzemski, Boston Red Sox's star outfielder. Somehow the inference was made that Tony C.'s problems stemmed from being traded. Moreover, Billy C. intimated that his problems with the Red Sox were largely a result of Yastrzemski's not liking him. Billy went on to explain that the reason Yastrzemski disliked the Conigliaros was because of some things they had said publicly about his having some canine qualities—he had violated that sacred baseball dictum, "Thou shalt run out everything thou layest wood on," at a game in Milwaukee the previous year.

Naturally, the newsmen ran for the door, trampling three unidentified brethren who were a bit slow of foot, to face Yastrzemski with the charge. Upon being confronted with the charges, Yaz replied, "I don't recall any incident in Milwaukee." Attaway, Carl, innocent all the way!

In any potential brouhaha such as this, particularly when the news media are involved and it is of such a nature that guilt cannot be proven at a later date, the wisest tactic to employ is to *play innocent*. Make it seem as if the other party is out of his head for even thinking such foul thoughts. It makes them look even more ridiculous than they are.

Of course, it should not pass unnoticed that the Conigliaros' tactics were disastrously chosen. What in the world could they possibly have gained by trying to shift the blame for their dismal performances onto the shoulders of Yastrzemski? So what if Yastrzemski didn't like them? So what if Yastrzemski did try to get them traded? All of these things are completely beside the point and Billy C. looked all the more pathetic in trying to pull down Yastrzemski, no matter how valid his case might have been.

Unfortunately, Yaz was unable to keep from becoming embroiled in the dispute. The next day he made a few comments about Billy C's performance, which, from a tactical standpoint, he probably shouldn't have made. The tactics he should have followed were to have stayed uninvolved in the whole hassle.

Refuse to get sucked into any name-calling situation. There is no percentage in it. There is no reward. Nothing is to be gained by engaging in such exchanges. If you feel the need for some satisfaction from such accusations, sit back and gloat about how much smarter you are than the other person in your wisdom to play it innocent all the way.

Piggyback

Fortune sometimes presents the manager an opportunity to get his way in several matters previously denied him by incorporating them as part of some other program for which he has gained approval.

One state legislature began to suspect that perhaps the strict line item budgeting system with which it had saddled its universities was not only wasteful but also impeded the educational process. Thus, it ordered one school in one university to install a Program Budgeting System for a year on an experimental basis. The dean of that school seized the opportunity to reorganize rather drastically both the school's curriculum and its departmental organization. Although neither of those administrative moves was really a necessary part of installing a Program Budgeting System, he made them seem so, thus tying them all together—he piggybacked his changes onto those requested by the legislature.

Two situations allow *piggybacking*. In the first case, the organization is willing to give the manager his desires as compensation for his cooperation—or, if you prefer, he is allowed to extort his programs as the price for his dedication to achieving the main goal.

In the other instance, the work group simply does not know what is going on. Thus it is in no position to question events. Whatever the leader says is accepted.

Put It in Writing

Suppose an adversary walks into your office with a sudden demand or plan about which you are either uncertain or opposed. One tactic is to ask him to put the *request in writing*. This gives you time to think about it, makes the adversary think through his position, possibly cools him off or encourages him to modify his demands, and it gets the adversary on paper—which may later prove to be highly advantageous because the document may prove to be his undoing.

As a general rule, having one's adversaries put plans or criticisms in writing is a very sound tactic. Sometimes merely requesting that a subordinate put something in writing thwarts his entire gambit. This can be either good or bad. It is bad if it stifles initiative or otherwise blocks off sound ideas.

It is particularly important to put the terms of any agreement down on paper. Oral agreements are notorious for their misunderstandings. After making an oral agreement, write a memo outlining what was agreed upon and send it to the other party. Certain advantages do accrue to the person who writes the memo, for he can to some extent shape the document to his advantage.

Conversely, one must be quite cautious in what he puts on paper, for it may be binding on him later. Never put anything in writing that you wouldn't want shown in court.

Do Something, No Matter What

President Nixon apparently had the *do something* tactic in his book of ploys. Certainly no economic illiterate, he knew full well not only the impossible problems posed by price and wage controls, but also the long run economic ineffectiveness of the measures. But something had to be done. The psychology of the situation demanded it. His moves were designed to assure the public and foreign money markets that we were concerned with our inflation.

The manager at times must knowingly take some ineffectual action as a symbol to his people that he cares. Perhaps it is nothing more than standing up to the boss by writing some memo to him protesting one thing or another.

A case could be made that ex-Los Angeles Rams coach Tommy Prothro failed to appreciate the usefulness of the do something tactic when the 1972 Rams were losing games that they should have won, largely because of their uninspired play. He kept insisting that a pro coach should not have to inspire intelligent, mature men who are professional football players. Perhaps that was so but something clearly needed to be done and he failed to perceive it. One cynical critic pointed to a flaw in Prothro's assumptions by asking, "What intelligent, mature man would be out there getting beat up each week?"

The faculty of one business school was upset over a change in the university's policy for faculty parking. Rare is the faculty that is content with parking—or much of anything else, for that matter. The point at issue was that the student parking lots were much closer to the business building than the faculty lot. The faculty wanted closer facilities and so apprised the dean at a meeting. The proper tactic would have been for the dean to promise the faculty that he would take the matter up with the president at the Deans' Council. But deans aren't famous for using the right tactics and this one in particular upheld the honor of his calling by replying, "You need the exercise." He dismissed the matter as trivial. It was not trivial to his people.

Go See the Wizard

Usually to be found in most large organizations are certain people who have been around so long, situated in jobs that bring them into contact with just about everyone in the organization, that they know who does what where.

The Johnny-come-lately to a large organization is severely hampered in his work from lack of knowledge about how to get things done and who to see. A new person should try to have assigned to him a secretary who knows her way around the corporation. One of the running jokes in a large lumber company was a certain woman of more than a few years and possessor of few skills whose continued longevity was attributed to knowledge of the corporation. She knew everyone, so she was automatically assigned to "wet nurse" new junior executives who needed contacts more than secretarial proficiency.

Thus, when you want to know something about the organization, *go see the wizard*—that is, the person who knows how to get things done. But wizards wear many masks. Some pose as experts or consultants; a few even know their calling. Even if one doesn't, he is not necessarily useless. If others believe he possesses powers, he may yet serve some purpose. Ed, an assistant to the president of a large consumer goods manufacturer, had been directed to make a "social audit" of the concern. Now Ed hadn't the foggiest idea of what one was, much less how to make one. For all he knew he might need a hammer and some nails. No matter—somewhere there had to be a Wizard of Social Audits. So off Ed went to the nearest citadel of higher learning in search of such a pundit. After a bit of nosing around Ed met a professor who professed he was an expert in making social audits. Ed had more than his share of doubts about the man, but he seemed to be the only wizard in town so he would have to do. And he did! The resulting report was buttressed with high sounding platitudes, spouting all the buzz words of the cult, and even a few well-turned phrases. It was roundly hailed by its intended audience, who had no basis to question it. When in the land of the blind, the man with one eye is king.

We should not leave this matter on such a cynical note because there are wizards whose talents can be of great use to those in need of them. It's a wise manager who recognizes when he needs a good wizard and knows where to find him.

Let's Do Research

One stalling tactic, which at times is unassailable, is to suggest that additional research needs to be done on a proposal. This always sounds so reasonable that many times it is difficult for the adversary to overcome it and get immediate action. Naturally many proposals die in the research stage where an adroit administrator can manage to have them buried by the selection of who is to *do the research* and how much is to be spent on it.

This tactic is kissing cousin to the stall tactic, but with a difference: there is a seemingly sound reason for this delay. It is surprising how many ideas are dampened by this maneuver, because the adversary is quite apt to write off further pursuit of his plan as being a waste of time. And he is probably correct, for the manager will most likely locate another tactic to forestall an unwanted plan.

"Let's make a survey!" is another well-worn stalling cliche. It takes time and can be designed to get whatever answers are wanted. If a survey is to be conducted, make certain you control it.

A four person committee was formed by the dean of a school of business to develop a program in entrepreneurship. Unfortunately, the chairman of the group was not in favor of such a program (history had shown him not to be in favor of much of anything that would require doing some work) on the basis that, in his opinion, there was no demand for it among the students. The fact that two sections of a course on new enterprises were overflowing and that some graduate students had asked for a seminar in new enterprises were not considered to be evidence of a demand by the chairman. No, a survey of the student body had to be made. So the proponents seized the reins of the survey, which was not at all difficult—remember, the adversary was lazy. You've got to know what that survey said.

The research ploy can also be used to pass the buck onto other shoulders. Ford was wont to blame its Edsel fiasco on faulty research, research that was largely ignored by management. A particularly costly, and most enterprising, program for marketing wood products by a large lumber company was in difficulty. Its project manager called for a research study to determine the difficulty. He hadn't the slightest intention of really listening to the study's findings and recommendations. Rather he was playing the standard game played by all executives in this company to cover themselves when called upon by the board of directors to explain their mismanagement of their program. Woe to the program manager who had not asked for research to assist him. But the manager who could show that he had done his homework, had the research performed, had no fear because he would be let off the hook as having done everything that could be expected of him. After all, if research can't save the day, how can mere mortals be expected to do better?

This love affair between the modern manager and research is so prevalent that more needs to be said about it. The intellectuals, in tacit conspiracy with the business press, have made research a religion. Woe to the manager who fails to pay homage to the new god—the researcher. Fortunately, there are some people who are beginning to question this cult.

The president of a rather large textile company was being severely pressed by many of his critics to spend some money on research. The firm did little research and none on basic fabrics. It had invented nothing. This fact was being used constantly against his administration. "They are backward." "How old fashioned can you get?" "Imagine, no research!" were but a few of the printable remarks made by corporate critics. Finally at a press conference at which he was being pressed on the matter he replied, "We have the biggest and finest research laboratories in the world. I call them DuPont, Monsanto, Chemstrand, and Dow." What he referred to was that the chemical companies and other large organizations were spending millions of dollars doing research, the results of which would be made available to his firm. He knew full well the futility of his company trying to duplicate the research efforts that were being expended in its behalf. Research costs a great deal of money and is a risky venture. Just doing research does not guarantee that profitable results will be forthcoming.

In the business area, little of what passes for research is of real use. We spend countless dollars studying things that are of no value. Look at the record of the research money being spent by several government agencies on incredible topics. While all of this sounds like heresy to the modern mind thoroughly indoctrinated with the research mystique, research is simply another business tool which must stand up to that rigid criteria of payoff—profit.

Keep a Key

One of the problems encountered by middle managers is that their thinking is frequently pirated by their superiors without due credit being given to the creator of the thoughts. A tactic to counter this theft is to *keep a key.* Keys come in many forms. One report writer quoted some important figures from a market study that was cited in a footnote. Guess who knew where the market study was to be found? Thus, the report's true author became known to top management. Make others come to you for the key, don't give it away.

One naive assistant not only wrote his boss's reports, but also gave him all of the supporting documents, even the work sheets. He had nothing to show for his efforts. There was no reason for the boss ever to consult him again on the matter.

A variation of the keep a key tactic entails making other people deal directly with you, rather than with someone else. An assistant was asked by his boss to survey the other vice-presidents about a matter. He could have asked them to reply to his boss, but he didn't. Instead, he asked that he be told their feelings.

Don't deal yourself out of the game.

Refer to a Committee

One of the classic stalling tactics is to refer a proposal or plan submitted by an adversary to a committee for further study. This can be an effective tactic to use, particularly when organizational policy clearly calls for it to be *given to some committee.* Committees can be an asset in helping the manager control the dimensions and characteristics of plans, if he has control over the membership of the committees.

If he does not have control over a committee, the use of this tactic can be risky, for he may not like the committee's recommendations. Also, this tactic can infuriate adversaries who are fully aware of what is going on. If their permanent alienation is not desirable, the use of this tactic may work to the long-run disadvantage of the manager. He can become known as a person who cannot make a decision for himself.

While we are discussing foot-dragging tactics some others are worthy of mention. An organization was meeting to plan a new budgeting system that it had been instructed to install by higher authorities. One department head, who was notorious for not wanting to do anything, proposed that the organization should first study its objectives, a move certain to spend a year leading only into a sea of platitudes and an ocean of frustration—a real stall. Fortunately, another department head rose to say, "If anyone here doesn't know our objectives, he should resign. We know what we're trying to do." The others chimed in and the stall was beaten. It takes guts to speak up against a study of objectives. One might as well come out against motherhood and the flag!

While critics of management have long decried the excessive use and misuse of committees, the practice still proliferates. In many organizations it is automatically assumed that a committee will be formed to do something or other when in fact it would make more sense to simply assign the task to one individual. However, there seems to be the thought adrift in our culture that somehow it is no longer permissible for an individual to do something. Everything must be a group effort, a group decision. Perhaps it is a collective age in which we now operate.

All of which is to say that not only are you free to use the committee tactic but indeed will be expected to do so in many organizations.

The provost at a large private university, the person who is in charge of all faculty, had been handed a hot potato by one of his weaker deans. It seems as if a ten-person tenure committee in the dean's school voted nine to one not to grant tenure to three professors who had been put up for that honor. Two of the three professors did the expected gentlemenly thing—they resigned. One decided he had not been given fair treatment and appealed. The dean had originally agreed with the tenure committee's decision but on appeal changed his mind. It might be added that the junior faculty members were greatly distressed over these tenure decisions because they obviously set standards that would be difficult for most of the younger people to meet. Thus the matter was dumped into the provost's lap for final decision.

As a matter of fact, as revealed to the writer by the provost himself, the provost completely agreed with the tenure committee. The man was undeserving of tenure. The provost had the power to make the final decision without consultation with anyone. However, he appointed a three man committee to advise him on the matter. One person was to be nominated by the professor, one by the dean, and one by the provost. Note that this committee was advisory only.

The provost was betting on the committee to make the decision that he wanted. If it worked out that way, then it would be a great tactic. If it did not, then the provost would have another problem: whether or not to override the committee. And that is one of the difficulties of using committees. One can never quite be sure of what they are going to do. Once done, the manager then is faced with a touchy problem of nullifying the committee's decision. Oh yes, the man was given tenure for it is dangerous to overrule committees.

Have a Fall Guy

It is usually best for one's career not to have the blood stains of a disaster fall directly on one's shoulders. Most plans of action entail some risk of disaster. In such cases, particularly where the risks are high, the wise manager may arrange to *have a scapegoat handy.* An executive vice-president of a manufacturing company was most interested in developing a certain new product that entailed considerable market risk. He spotted a bright young junior executive who was also highly interested in the product and let the young man believe that the product's idea was his own and that it would provide the young man with a tremendous opportunity for advancement in the organization, should he be able to pull off the new product introduction successfully. When the product failed, no criticism was aimed at the executive vice-president since he was apparently free from direct responsibility. He had seen to it that the entire responsibility for the new product rested on the shoulders of the product manager who, for some odd reason, found himself seeking new employment.

This tactic has little risk if it is done with sufficient subtlety. Success in most large corporations depends upon the adept execution of this tactic, for the key to advancement is to never be left holding the bag for some corporate disaster. If one can just keep his nose clean for the requisite number of years, his advancement is assured.

One of the difficulties that beset Nixon was that the people who should have been the natural fall guys were unwilling to play the role. They refused to take the rap but instead started pointing fingers at other people—thus they all were indicted.

The care and feeding of fall guys can be a delicate matter. Most of the time one need not be concerned with taking care of the fall guy, because he may not be a willing player. At other times, though, a person may agree to be the fall guy in exchange for some protection or payoff. Historically, fall guys who come to feel they have been badly treated have caused whatever trouble they could—and at times that trouble has been considerable when the matter has some public interest.

Control the Environment—Bestow the Status Symbols

Let there be no doubt about it, *status symbols* are terribly important to just about everyone, whether or not they maintain otherwise. The person from whom the symbols flow is held in esteem and deference. Delegate such bestowal rights and you have given your subordinate new, rather substantial power in the organization. The organization will toady to the person from whom the favors flow. And the manager should not shy from withholding his favors from those people whose behavior displeases him. Should he refrain from exercising his power, others will feel freer to deviate from desired paths. Moreover, it should be made abundantly clear to the subordinate that the symbols he seeks are being granted as a reward for his dedication and loyalty.

One new plant manager, upon assuming his responsibilities, encountered an immediate subordinate—the personnel manager—who proved to be a rather disruptive factor at executive committee meetings. He talked too much and said too little. What he did say the manager did not want to hear, nor did he want anyone else to hear it, for they were thoughts not conducive to the programs the new manager wanted to institute.

At first, the personnel manager's office was next to the manager's and they shared the same outer office. That arrangement did not last for long; the personnel manager was moved to a remote area for a contrived reason. Other symbols were stripped from him. The organization got the word—cooperate or else.

Exile to Siberia

Sometimes a manager is in a position to physically move an adversary—*exile him*—so that he is rendered relatively impotent. At times this can be done by disguising it as a promotion. The adversary is offered a promotion to some remote spot in the organization where he will cause the manager little future trouble.

The dean of one school of business was bothered by one troublesome professor who was continually creating one problem or another. Inasmuch as the university had several campuses and it was completely within the dean's discretion to determine the man's teaching assignment, he simply assigned the man to a remote, small campus, thereby isolating him geographically.

Sometimes being exiled does not require a geographical move but merely an organizational one. The top management of a large corporation had a particularly troublesome middle management man who was too aggressive for their conservative tastes. Since the man had an outstanding record of productivity, they could not fire him without many questions being asked. However, his immediate superior conned him into accepting a promotion to head up a troublesome division of the company that was a quagmire containing the remains of many promising managerial careers. After doing an admirable job with the division, the young executive finally became fed up with its unsolvable problems and resigned, to the silent relief of the conservative higher management.

One of the most painful evenings the author can recall was spent at the home of a friend who was giving a good-bye dinner for a friend of his who was being transferred from Colorado to North Dakota by his employer, a large map publishing company. Since everyone assumed that he was being promoted, the usual questions concerning his new position were asked. It became rather embarrassingly evident that the man had been given the choice of either being fired or exiled. His new job was distinctly inferior to the one he had and he left no question about his desire not to go. But he had no viable alternative since he was in his late fifties and had no other skills to sell in the job market.

Conclusion

There is possibly no limit to the number of different tactics and variations thereof that you can observe in action around you. Each incident requires some modification of tactics, and on occasion the manager must create some new maneuver to handle the matter at hand. Certainly tactical behavior should not be considered a static, closed system. Clever managers develop new tactics with which to handle new problems. It is hoped that the material in this book has furnished you with some ideas of the scope of managerial tactics and their potential usefulness. Moreover, it is hoped that you will now be more aware of the tactics that are constantly being used by the managers around you. Finally, perhaps this material will somehow enable you to accomplish what you are trying to do. (Whatever that is!)

3

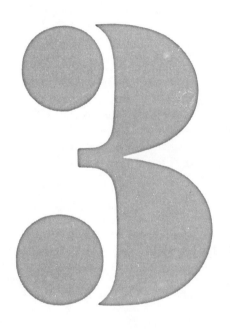

Tactics Involving Personal Relationships

some people call it politics

Many of the daily tactics the manager uses concern his relationships with his subordinates, peers, and superiors. Indeed, his success in the organization is largely determined by how adroitly he handles these relationships because if he fails to develop them properly he is lost.

Usually the manager is friendly with his peers for they are really the only people in the organization with whom he can socialize comfortably. But one can encounter problems with peer relationships. There are always competitive jealousies lurking on the horizon that one must guard against. And then there is the manager who is on the way up and knows it. He had better not form too close of a relationship with those of his peers who one day will be his subordinates. Ever fire a friend, discipline a buddy? Personal involvement with one's subordinates inserts an element into the decision process that warps the results. The able administrator must carefully select his peer group friends. Pick the winners, avoid the losers. You are judged by the company you keep. Associate with the people who are going places and doing things.

People are frequently unhappy that they are unable to develop the close personal relationships with others that they had during their school years; but the gloried, innocent days of childhood are largely a product of a wistful memory.

Although many superiors encourage close relationships with their subordinates, from the subordinate's viewpoint the relationship is difficult and dangerous. He is on the spot constantly and must be careful of everything he says and does. Moreover, should the subordinate try to make too much of the personal relationship or capitalize on it, he may discover that the boss's goodwill was not what he had been led to believe.

Friendliness on the part of the boss is often misconstrued. It may just be his natural personality or an effort on his part to get to know his people better, to be human. He may not intend that it go any further.

One particular personality flaw in some superiors causes great grief to unsuspecting subordinates. This flaw belongs to the boss who openly develops a close relationship with a subordinate and then inevitably turns on him when he decides the subordinate does not meet his standards of perfection—and no one can meet them. These are bosses you keep away from, lest they destroy you. Familiarity does breed contempt in people who are incapable of accepting others as they are, faults and all.

The person who develops a close relationship with his boss will be subject to a certain amount of resentment, and various tactics will be used against him by others in the organization who are either jealous or who want to destroy the relationship.

Admittedly, there are superiors who are lonely. They crave a close relationship with somebody, somebody in whom they can place trust, somebody who can act as a sounding board, somebody who can be a playmate. It is dangerous for a subordinate to try to play this role; only in rare instances will it work out successfully.

And then there are the bosses who demand that subordinates keep their distance, call them "Mister," treat them with exaggerated respect. If this describes your boss, then you should be most circumspect in your contacts with him. There are far more of these people around than is obvious on the surface, because modern social pressures have forced such traditionalists to change their outward behavior. Do not be deceived by their apparent behavior, for at heart they still want the symbols of respect they think are due people in their position. Give it to them!

And now what about your subordinates? There are advantages to being close to those under you. You have better communications with them and can evaluate them more accurately. They should respond to your leadership more readily. But what is "close?" Where does "close" stop and "intimate" begin? It is a most difficult line to draw, but it must be drawn. There are grave dangers awaiting the boss who becomes an intimate friend with a subordinate. One of the problems is that one cannot be equally close to all of his subordinates, so inevitably some of them feel discriminated against. The answers to these questions depend upon a good many factors, such as the personalities of the boss and the employees, their relative social backgrounds, the size of the organization, and the caliber of the employees.

As you can now see, I have no answers to these questions of your personal relationships in business, only warnings and a few observations.

The academic world calls this interpersonal relationships. The losers tend to call it politics, while the winners prefer to think of it as getting along with people. Whatever one calls it, there is a field of knowledge and endeavor which is concerned with how the individual gains the favor of other people from whom he wants things. We want all sorts of things: prestige, money, position, power, and respect. Some people seem to know how to get these things better than other people. Traditionally, these goodies are supposed to reward those who possess the greatest talent, the greatest intellect, or the greatest expertise. But observation has disillusioned those who hold that virtue will win in the end. The winners seem to be those people who are most adept at politics; that is, at the art of manipulating other people.

There are those who would say, "So what! What's so wrong about our leadership slots being filled by adept politicians?" Plenty! Such people are not the best at doing the jobs they are supposed to do. Many are even incompetent in the technical aspects of their jobs. Not many people would care to be operated on by a brain surgeon who holds his job because he is the most adept politician in the hospital.

Care to fly in airplanes built by people who are not technically competent? Yet that is exactly the dilemma with which our culture is faced today. We are led by people who are where they are because of their political skills, not because they are best fitted for the job.

Since there is no practical way this can be altered, it then behooves those people who possess great technical abilities to become sufficiently skilled politicians that they can assume their rightful place. We suffer a great loss when some outstandingly talented person is so inept in his personal relationships that he is prevented from contributing his talents to society.

Thus my plea is rather simple. Since it is not possible to remove politics from the reward system, then it is important that those people who have talent learn to play the game, learn to use it to their advantage.

Loyalty

While it might seem odd to some people that *loyalty* should be considered a managerial tactic, a bit of thought discloses that it most certainly is one, and a most effective one at that. Loyalty is a characteristic highly prized by most executives. Indeed, your boss can forgive a great many shortcomings in your character and capabilities, but seldom will he forgive your disloyalty. Most people interpret disloyalty as a personal affront to their entire existence. On the other hand, there are innumerable cases that have been brought to light where incompetent people have been able to successfully rise in business solely because they have been able to prove their loyalty to a superior whose star was rising. They rose as his career rose. A bit of analysis quickly discloses the reason for this phenomenon. Consider for a moment the opposite situation. How can an executive possibly have anyone around him or associated with him whom he distrusts, whose loyalty he cannot count upon? A disloyal person can do a great deal of damage and everyone knows it.

The slightest indication that a subordinate is not totally loyal is immediate grounds for getting rid of him or at least placing him in a position that minimizes his opportunities to do mischief.

But since loyalty seems to be such a continuous affair, how can it be a specific tactic? Very simply! There arise certain occasions in which the manager is able to demonstrate his loyalty unquestionably—loyalty to his people or loyalty to the organization. Those are times when he does something solely out of loyalty to someone other than himself, something he didn't have to do, or even something he shouldn't have done other than for reasons of loyalty. Adversity is the test of loyalty. Is the individual there and does he stand up to be counted when the going gets rough? We all know quite well that most people fail this acid test, but people have a tendency to remember those who remember them when they're down.

First, let's take a look at a case of disloyalty. The treasurer of a certain city had an assistant who, for years, was loyal and diligent in her efforts. But there came a time when the treasurer began a feud with the city's new mayor, of whom the assistant thought a great deal. The assistant felt that her superior was definitely wrong in a great many things he was doing to make life miserable for the mayor; so she proceeded to keep the mayor informed of all her superior's maneuvers. Eventually the treasurer became aware of her disloyalty and fired her. Thereupon she appealed to the mayor for a job elsewhere. The mayor could not find an opening for his spy. Spies have a difficult time in this world; no one can quite trust them.

On the other hand, there is the case of a young assistant sales manager whose boss became the victim of company politics largely through his own bullheadedness. While the assistant did not agree with many things the sales manager had done, he still felt that the man had many significant virtues and thus should go far in the business world. Moreover, the assistant felt certain that his advancement in the company was definitely limited; he would not be given the sales manager's job. When the sales manager left for greener pastures, the assistant asked to go with him. The sales manager was so gratified at such a sign of loyalty (what executive doesn't harbor the desire to take everyone with him he can. "I'll show the world just what a rotten mess they have here.") The sales manager offered his assistant a position with a handsome increase in salary. The two made an effective team thereafter.

Thus it can be seen that while loyalty is taken for granted, the individual who manages to demonstrate his loyalty above and beyond the call of duty is frequently rewarded disproportionately.

Work

Work—what some people consider to be the dirtiest four-letter word of all—is a most effective tactic, one not used nearly enough. Many careers have been built on the ability to project to superiors the idea that one is an extremely hard worker. And it is not always a matter of output. One can have a great deal of output, perhaps more than anyone else in the organization, and yet be considered lazy if he doesn't look like he is putting out the effort. For some reason, people feel that there is a great deal of virtue in just the appearance of putting a lot of effort into the job. Productivity is only appreciated by the more sophisticated individuals in the organization. Thus the adept manager quickly learns the importance of appearing to be busy, of coming to work early in the morning, leaving late at night, working on weekends, and always creating lots of action. Of course, many of these appearances are merely smoke screens.

The president of one of the nation's largest companies publicly boasts in print of getting to work every morning at 7:30. That's true! He also leaves at 11:00 A.M. to go to the club to enjoy an afternoon's round of golf. He returns to the office by closing time for everyone to see him busily engaged as they leave. Most of his employes really believe he is a hard worker. Having been his golf companion, I know better.

While the astute superior will try to evaluate his subordinates on the basis of their output, in practice this is difficult to do because there may be no measurable output in the short run against which to judge the person. Thus appearances must suffice. The person who uses work as a basic tactic always disguises his pleasurable activities with the cloak of economic endeavor. He never goes on a vacation, he's in the field visiting dealers. He never plays golf, he's out making a customer contact. He never goes to the theater, he's entertaining customers. Don't delude yourself about the effectiveness of this tactic. Few things rile up one's peers so much as an apparent ability to do one's work with far less effort than they must expend to do theirs. The person to whom work comes easily must endeavor to make it look otherwise. Of course, one must use some judgment in the matter, for people who are always talking about how hard they work become not only very boresome but also an organizational joke. Actions are what are required, not words.

Of course, we should not leave this topic without pointing out that those people who sincerely work hard at their jobs usually realize far more success in life than those who don't—contrary to the observations most losers make about life.

Avoid Losers

An old adage advises that *one is judged by the company he keeps,* and observation supports that advice. Successful people definitely tend to flock together, as do losers. If you insist on being mentally and visually associated with people who are considered incompetent, you may be similarly judged. It is most important that one avoid being connected with people who are known to be on the wrong side of the political fence in an organization. While this advice seems obvious, its execution is made difficult because losers actively seek association with new people in an organization. They go out of their way to recruit the new person into their group, thus placing a burden upon him to be careful about whom he associates with initially. An individual should project an image that he is successful, for few things breed success like success. Lest you doubt this unpopular philosophy, all you have to do is be in a position someday to look successful in your mode of living and then observe what starts happening. People suddenly know you. The mail is filled with invitations to various affairs, all usually requiring some investment on your part. Business propositions of all sorts will be laid at your doorstep. You will have options that you did not have previously. Then, make it known that in fact you are not the prosperous person you projected, if your ego is up to it.

Aside from the image considerations there are some far more worthy aspects to this matter. You can not grow with losers. You may learn a little about how to lose but that is a lesson easily had on any street corner. Winners can teach you many things, most importantly how to win. Things happen around winners. If you're around, the same things may happen to you, but don't count on it. Instead, count on their impact on your mental attitude. Get the winning attitude and you'll be more likely to win.

Put Salve on Their Wounds

In the normal course of bureaucratic affairs, all participants suffer battle damage and various cuts and bruises to their managerial egos. Sometimes the manager inflicts the damage; other times he is an innocent bystander.

Jerry, a young product manager for a large package goods manufacturer, called long distance to a business acquaintance whom he considered a friend. The reason for his call was ostensibly a good one, but the conversation quickly turned to Jerry's problems with his superiors. It developed that an extensive organizational shakeup was underway and that while Jerry's job was not in jeopardy, several of his pet products were being taken away from him and given to another division. Moreover, he felt that he had been treated rather badly in other respects. He asked directly if his friend knew of any other jobs in the industry but his friend said he didn't.

Then the friend got out the old bucket of salve and began massaging it into Jerry's wounds. "Jerry, don't do anything hasty. I know they regard you highly. After all, if your services weren't valued, you would have been given your walking papers in this shakeup. Any time you have organizational realignments on such a massive scale everyone is bound to come out with hurt feelings because they think they are being given the runaround. It's just that the people doing the shuffling haven't got time to think about or consider your personal feelings. They're fighting bigger problems. So just hold tight. Don't do anything rash. It'll all work out. You've got a good job and you're doing a good job. Stick with it!"

This dialogue was all pure hogwash. The man was doing a bad job and his "friend" didn't tell him of known job vacancies because he was unwilling to recommend him for them. But for purely selfish reasons, the "friend" could not risk alienating Jerry, because he was still in a position to do him great harm (refer to the tactic, don't burn your bridges, which stresses this point).

Sometimes it is even more important to make liberal use of the salve jar when you have personally inflicted the damage. Ease the pain a bit. Liberal severance pay and other termination benefits are common salves applied to people who have been fired. Offers to help a discharged employee find employment elsewhere similarly soothes ruffled feelings. It discourages the discharged person from saying or doing unpleasant things out of fear that the salve will be withheld. The basic idea is to place the discharged person in the position of losing even more than his job if he behaves badly about being fired.

Pour Oil on Troubled Waters

Whereas the previous tactic of putting salve on wounds referred to the treatment of individuals' troubles, *pouring oil on troubled waters* refers to the treatment of situations involving groups of people. It is an age-old tactic which managers have frequent occasion to use. Not only is it safe to use, but usually well-advised.

Normal day-to-day operations give rise to problems, injured feelings, damaged egos, threatened positions, disputes, jealousies—you name it. As a manager, you may be approached by your subordinates, peers, or even superiors who are upset over something or other. Most of the time it is best to pour oil on troubled waters to try to avoid further conflict in the organization because seldom does conflict produce much good. A calm, dispassionate hand-holder is usually able to bring the aggravated party back to rationality.

A vice-president's office staff became visibly upset one afternoon over the activities of some people from the company's personnel office who were interviewing everyone in the office about their jobs, what they did, what they were paid, and so forth. This distressed the vice-president for he had not been told of the visits. To neglect to tell the VP was not only against company policy but was also not good management practice. He too was troubled, but for different reasons. However, he did not let on to the secretary who came to him with the story. Rather he poured oil on the riled sea. "There is absolutely nothing to worry about. The personnel department is just making a study of jobs and their difficulty in an attempt to equate pay with the tasks. No one will suffer." He was saying all this not from positive knowledge about the matter but rather from the strength he knew he possessed to stop any unwise personnel practices. He simply had faith that some fathead in personnel had undertaken some such study in fulfillment of Parkinson's Law. Investigation (a phone call) proved that this was so. The personnel manager was properly chastised by top management for undertaking the study without clearing it with the people concerned. There were other vice-presidents who were similarly angry at the unnecessary troubles that had been caused.

A marketing manager for a food products concern had lost several of his people to an aggressive competitor who had pirated them away by offering them more money. At an industry trade show, he was sounding off rather loudly about certain "unethical" scoundrels who were stealing "his" people. He loudly ordered his competitor to stay away from "his" people.

The competitor just smiled and let the man rave, adding a little fuel to the fire now and then by saying something like, "You know, that man McDonald of yours sure looks good. I think I'll go after him."

The marketing manager was near rage when a good friend of

his pulled him into the hall, admonishing him, "You're making a fool of yourself! You don't own those people. There is nothing I can think of that you can do to drive your people away from you faster than to try to hold onto them the way you're going about it. If you try to prevent their getting outside offers, they will wash their hands of you."

Pouring oil on troubled waters worked. The man later thanked his friend profusely for the advice. For some reason he had lost control of his emotions and needed an outside party to bring him back to even keel.

4

Timing Tactics

Timing is of the essence in the maneuvers of most managers. Deciding when to take action can be just as critical in the final outcome of a plan as the substance of the plan itself. And so consideration must be given to timing tactics.

Underlying most timing tactics is the matter of the mental attitude of one's adversaries. A person's reaction to any action is heavily conditioned by all the things that have happened to him previously, particularly in the immediate past. If the boss's wife has just filed suit for divorce, it is not the time to ask him for a raise or for much of anything else.

There are some general observations that can be made on factors that affect timing decisions. Admittedly, these are no more than common sense, but for the sake of completeness they are included here.

Economic outlook is a vital factor. When a person (or an organization) feels no money pressures, he is usually much more susceptible to your tactics. Moreover, wealth tends to dull one's tactical finesse.

The amount of the adversary's involvement in other affairs will affect his reaction to your tactical behavior. A busy person may not care to become involved.

Students of the stock market well know that timing is everything. There is always a time to sell and a time to buy and one's profits are determined by how well the investor recognizes those times.

There are good times to launch new ventures and there are bad times to do so. A large new Chevrolet dealership opened in Dallas right in the midst of the depressed car market of 1975; it has yet to even come close to making money.

Unfortunately one's timing tactics are not usually unrestricted. In many instances you aren't free to decide when to do something. Professional investment managers, the people who manage millions of dollars for other people, are prisoners of the money which they must invest. There were times in the immediate past when they would have much preferred to remain uninvested—that is, to stay in cash. But they could not liquidate their huge portfolios. There was no one to buy them. Thus their situations force them to forego many timing considerations. Their problem is not one of when to invest but rather in what to invest.

Implicit in using the tactic of *letting the situation worsen* timing is the question—how bad does the situation have to get before I do something? Such judgment decisions can not be intelligently covered because they depend entirely on the situation, and only the person on the spot can evaluate all the factors at work.

Later it will be mentioned that patience is a virtue that one must cultivate in becoming a skilled negotiator. The person who is impatient will give away too much value in his quest for an early settlement. Again, patience is a timing phenomenon—when should one act? The discounted present value of future benefits is the culprit counseling the impatient person. There are real values in settling matters quickly. For one thing less effort is needed. Thus the manager is freed to attend to other things. The passage of time always inserts additional risks into any affair. Things can happen that will place one at an even greater disadvantage in the bargaining. Thus the manager is torn between the virtue of patience and the virtue of swift action. Again, there is an indeterminate equation here for everything depends upon the person's evaluation of the situation at hand.

Thus we can conclude that the manager's timing decisions are significantly affected by five forces: (1) the risks inherent in the situation, (2) the confidence he has in his information, (3) the accuracy of his forecasts, (4) the likelihood that the matter may be self healing, and (5) the direction of affairs.

Where do the large risks lie? Perhaps waiting exposes one to the risk. Or the risks may lie in acting too fast. What is the safest timing tactic? Perhaps an analogy can be used from medicine. A person who has been told that he suffers from a serious cancer is not inclined to wait for treatment. The risks lie in waiting too long and are minimized by prompt attention to the ailment. On the other hand, you are told that you require some minor surgery but now suffer from an unrelated respiratory condition (you have a bad cold!). The doctor decides it best to wait until your cold clears up before operating on you. The biggest risk here is in immediate action.

Uncertainty about one's information usually delays decision making. Generally the manager prefers to have better information before making a decision or taking an action. Acting quickly on bad information does little for careers.

Most decisions are implicitly based on some sort of forecast of future events. The manager carries around with him at all times a rather complex and lengthy number of forecasts about what is going to happen in the future. Typically, the individual who is uncertain of the future tends to act in the present. The more confident one is about what will happen in the future, the clearer he will see what timing action is appropriate.

If there is a likelihood that the problem will take care of itself, then the manager is likely to wait and let it have a chance to do so. Why act if it is not necessary?

Are matters getting better or worse? The labor negotiator who prolongs a contract negotiation when the company's fortunes are waning has reason to worry about his tactics. On the other hand, if a big increase in profits is to be announced shortly, perhaps the labor leader would be wise to stall until after the announcement. Kaiser Wilhelm surrendered quickly when the tide clearly turned against him, thus minimizing his losses; Hitler refused to do so, consequently causing great grief for his people.

Leave Well Enough Alone

It takes a manager of great wisdom and patience to be able to keep his hands off a situation that is bothering him; but sometimes that is precisely what he must do—nothing. Sometimes this is the proper tactic to use because nothing can be done about a situation. The manager is helpless to correct it and his meddling will do nothing but worsen the situation or jeopardize his position. In other cases the matter is none of his affair. It is the responsibility of some other manager and he had better not interfere.

Sometimes a situation is such that it is simply not serious enough to warrant the manager's spending his time with it. For the sake of efficiency, he should leave it alone. This is particularly true in situations where the amount of time required would be relatively large in comparison with the profits that could be achieved. Calvin Coolidge once said, "If ten troubles come down the road at you and you just stand still, nine of them will fall by the wayside and you'll only have to deal with the one that reaches you." Some problems take care of themselves. A troublesome employee may resign, retire, or request a transfer.

Sometimes the manager may not be happy about some action or program developed by a subordinate, but he should refrain from interfering with it for three reasons: (1) allowing subordinates freedom without interference can facilitate their development and growth; (2) there is no assurance that the manager's thoughts will be superior to those of the subordinate; and (3) the program is apt to be more successful if the people responsible for implementing it have developed it.

A leading salesman for a large furniture manufacturer had been promoted to sales manager. He had been aware of several problems in the alignment of sales territories. While he wanted to straighten out the sales territories, he wisely deferred this action because it was not really hurting sales volume. Furthermore, to juggle the territorial boundaries upon assumption of his managership might have caused some moral problems and jeopardized some other programs he wished to institute.

The manager must take care that the problems he leaves alone will not later become uncontrollable or unmanageable. The president of a large university had a problem with an editor of the student newspaper who insisted on printing articles libeling various important people. In the name of academic freedom, the president refrained from acting until he was forced to do so. He eventually fired the editor, but it was too late to save his own job because he was also fired shortly thereafter.

A manager may have to act in spite of his belief that he should *leave well enough alone.* If his organization feels that something definitely must be done about a situation, he may have to make some moves for reasons of morale. However, these moves may be but token efforts to placate his people.

An organization was saddled with a lame duck employee for six months. To the discomfort of two peers, the lame duck insisted on playing his regular role in the organization rather than assuming the usual role of a lame duck. The two let it be known to the boss that he should speak with the lame duck about his proper role. The boss was amused with the situation and saw no need for action. He was happy that the lame duck was not causing any real problems and wished to keep it that way. But he placated his two men by agreeing to "have a talk with" the lame duck. They talked—about the lame duck's plans and how the boss could be of help to him!

Choose Your Time

Timing is critical in the execution of most plans. In fact, a case can be made that the success or failure of any gambit may depend more upon its timing than upon any other single factor. An executive wishes to hire a highly capable person away from a competitor. Whether or not he gets that person may depend upon the timing of his proposition. Almost inevitably there are times in anyone's life when he will be receptive to job offers.

Obviously the administrator attempts to choose a time in which the adversary is either most susceptible to suggestion or a time when he is unable to defend himself.

A businessman may be unwilling to negotiate some financial matter in realistic terms at a time when he feels prosperous, but should his fortunes turn for the worse he may be far more reasonable in his demands. The converse may also be true, depending on his personality. One white-collar worker learned that a bank had just given a local car dealer an ultimatum to clear out some car inventory that had been in stock far too long. He was able to approach the dealer immediately and buy a new car on quite advantageous terms, whereas three months previously the dealer had been unreasonable in his price demands. Timing is frequently everything in price negotiations.

Sometimes the timing tactic is closely akin to the stall. In stalling, the manager does everything in his power to prolong an affair, because the situation may be such that with the passing of time he gains bargaining power. Either his strength is increasing or the adversary's is decreasing. One large automobile dealer, in advising a fellow dealer about a dispute with a bank over some installment paper that went bad, said, "Everytime I have a hassle with my banker, I just make a mental note that we'll settle it in about three years. There is no hurry about it. Just don't take any action at all. Let the bank initiate all the action and do all the moving. You remain passive. They'll keep kicking it around between junior executives, with each one taking about six months to do anything, and before you know it three years have passed and somebody down there will make up his mind that they had better settle it. So they'll come to you and will be quite reasonable. But if you rush in trying to get this thing settled, you'll lose your advantage.

It is only good sense to act when it is advantageous to do so and avoid acting when it is to the adversary's advantage. Time can favor either party, depending upon the circumstances. Sometimes you will want to push for quick action, other times you will want to delay. But bear in mind that time inserts additional risks into the affair.

A businessman wanted to buy a certain building from one of his acquaintances. The owner was only slightly unrealistic in his price. They were $3,000 apart so the buyer decided to wait out the seller, confident that he really wanted to sell but was just being a tough negotiator. The seller, on the other hand, saw no need to rush into the sale. His property was sound and he was getting a good rent on it. Why not wait for a "good" price? So he did. In this case both parties chose the correct tactic. The buyer found another property at a more attractive price and the seller found a more willing buyer.

In an almost identical case, both lost. The buyer ended up paying more, because of inflation, for an inferior property; and the seller's tenant went bankrupt, thus causing a great loss of rent, what's worse, the subsequent operator of the firm was unwilling to pay as much rent. Inasmuch as the owner had no immediate alternative, he had to take the deal.

Time is risk. Take the risk of waiting when the potential gains seem worthwhile.

Be Patient

Recently an outstanding lawyer voiced this opinion in a casual conversation: "I believe, that in all my legal experience with business probably the single most important virtue a good businessman can have is *patience*. Many things simply take time and the man who is impatient inevitably commits mistakes to his disadvantage. It takes time to build empires and get things done and the impatient man is at a distinct disadvantage." Good advice!

This tends to be particularly applicable to young businessmen who are impatient to get ahead with things. They are constantly figuring out ways to accomplish things in a short while and becoming impatient with those who seem to slow them down. It takes time to get situations straightened around and clarified. Many times the winner in a contest is the one who outlives the other, or outstays him. Many older executives simply bury their adversaries. A dean of a school of business took over a situation in which several older professors were thorns in his side, delaying several progressive programs he would have liked to begin. However, he decided that since the men were near retirement age most of his problems would be solved within five years. Rather than risking a frontal attack in the situation, he simply bided his time until they retired, and then he went ahead with his programs.

Unfortunately, time is of the essence; and while biding one's time, opportunities can be lost forever and one adversary can be substituted for another. Patience may be the mask of the timid person.

Mr. Clements, chief executive officer of the Dr. Pepper company, in an impromptu speech accepting the Southern Methodist University's award as an outstanding businessman, made special mention of the role of patience in his success. He said that countless times in the past he could have easily become impatient with this or that and have done something that would have drastically altered his career. But he didn't—and so he finally arrived at the top of his calling. It is all too easy for talented people to become impatient with their advancement or with the shortcomings of their associates and do some rash thing that hurts their long run interests. Patience and tolerance are close cousins because one must be tolerant to be patient.

Let the Situation Worsen

Occasionally the best one can do is to *let a bad situation get worse*, for if he acts too soon he will be criticized as taking unwarranted action. President Roosevelt had to use this tactic in instituting rationing during World War II. He had to let the situation deteriorate until the public would accept rationing; if he had acted any earlier, he would have encountered considerable resistance from the public.

There are some dangers in using this tactic, for some situations may worsen to the point where a manager cannot straighten out the mess, thereby causing losses. It takes great forbearance to let a situation worsen to a point where action can be taken. A sales manager had a salesman in a particularly critical territory who had been one of the company's leading performers at one time, but who had been slipping steadily in recent years. This salesman had many friends throughout the company and was well liked. Though the sales manager, from a strictly managerial standpoint, had ample reason to discharge the man for his failing performance, to do so would have created a serious morale problem in the organization. He was forced to sit by for two years until the man's performance became so shoddy that everyone in the organization was aware of it. When the sales manager finally discharged the man, the organization's general consensus was, "Why wasn't it done earlier?"

Two senior executives in a large charitable organization were concerned with the public behavior of the head of the organization. During the past year he had constantly been on the road obstensibly raising money; but it appeared to some that he was running for public office. He had left his executive secretary in charge of daily operations. Unfortunately, the organization had developed several serious problems which were not being attended to. The employees were complaining about a lack of leadership—the program was drifting. Moreover, far too much of the money was being spent on administration instead of welfare. There were too many people sitting around the headquarters doing things that did not need doing.

Mr. A aked Mr. B his opinion of what, if anything, they should do about the situation. Mr. B replied, "At the present time there is nothing we can do about it. It is a problem for the board of directors to handle when they finally realize what is going on. If we try to do anything now we will only ruin our chances of stepping in later to play an important role in reforming the organization." Mr. A agreed. They did nothing but let the situation worsen. And it did! Within the month the board removed the head and put Mr. A in charge of the clean up.

Strike While the Iron Is Hot

This age-old tactic almost speaks for itself. The aggressive, alert manager must *strike when it is highly advantageous* for him to do so, regardless of all other factors, because the success of his plan may depend more upon the existence of fortunate timing than any other factor in the situation.

Naturally, the manager must make certain that the time is right and that when he strikes he has sufficient resources with which to do the job. A fifty-five year old treasurer of a medium-sized corporation was offered the controllership of a large, prestigious organization. He hesitated and then turned it down. Within a few months the situation in his company was completely altered by a merger. He contacted the larger firm again, only to find that they were no longer interested in him. Apparently neither was anyone else, so he had to stay in an unhappy situation.

This timing tactic is probably responsible for more fortunes than any other tactic. Most successful operators have the knack of sensing the right time to act. They see opportunity and seize it. Examples are so numerous and obvious that no purpose is served by citing them here. However, a warning is needed. Reference to this tactic is frequently made by scoundrels to rush naive people into bad deals. There are a great many opportunities that will wait, that do not need to be seized. One successful businessman claimed, "I have found no shortage of opportunities. Sure, I've missed out on some good deals by going slow. I have also saved myself a great deal of grief by passing up some bad ones. I believe in another adage: 'Look before you leap!' "

Strike When You're Strong

The manager is wise if he postpones making his move until he is sufficiently strong or ready to execute it successfully. The president of a small university particularly desired to build up a doctoral program in one of the sciences, but he had to delay introduction of his program for three years while he was garnering manpower and resources to make the program successful when introduced. To have announced the program earlier and to have accepted students into it would have jeopardized its long run success.

However, some of the famous military disasters in history were caused by leaders who waited and waited until they felt they were sufficiently strong for the plan at hand; they were undone by the delay. Timid leaders frequently like to use this tactic as a cover up for their timidity in instances where such strength is really not necessary for the plan. One seldom has the resources he thinks he should have to execute a plan successfully.

In some instances one has the strongest position early in his tenure on the job. Your superiors are more apt to grant you your requests when you are fresh on the job than later when you will be treated like one of the mob. The chairman of the board of a large publishing house was counseling a close friend of his who was negotiating for a vice-presidency of another publishing concern. He admonished, "Get your money before you accept the job. Hold their feet to the fire now. You won't be able to do it later." The reason for this is logical. Once you have accepted employment with an organization there is a natural inertia that keeps you in that job. You are not likely to up and quit because you are not given this or that. So if you want this or that, then get it while you are still free and they want you. In many situations your strongest bargaining position comes before you commit yourself. Perhaps the pledging rituals of college fraternities are a good case in point. One famous professional football player was relating his experiences as a graduating senior and second round draft choice of a contending NFL team. While the team was trying to sign him, he could do no wrong. They treated him like royalty. Once he signed, "I was dog meat."

A new president took the reins of leadership of a sizable

manufacturing company that had suffered badly from a long string of presidents who lacked whatever it took to make the operation profitable. The new man was most promising. After he disclosed his plans to a close friend, he was advised, "Do it quickly. Get the board's approval for everything right now. Don't wait! Right now you have great strength. They can not refuse you because they cannot stand another search for a president. But wait for awhile and those buzzards will work on you. They will grow increasingly disenchanted with you and your programs no matter how well they are doing. That has been their nature." Good advice!

All Bets are Made on the First Tee

Golfers of any betting sophistication realize that the outcome of most bets is determined on the first tee. The winners and the losers are determined more by those first tee negotiations than by the skills displayed on the course. Give away too many strokes to a sandbagging hustler and you can shoot the lights out yet lose the rent money.

The businessman who yields to the labor leader's unjustifiably high demands will pay for his folly from that point on. He will not be able to call off the deal later, any more than the losing golfer can scream about handicaps on the 17th hole. *All bets are made on the first tee.*

If you make a bad deal with someone, seldom is there much that you can do to salvage the situation. Thus make certain that the deals you make are sound from the beginning. A contract is a contract and few are renegotiable. Agree to pay too much rent for a store and you're probably stuck with it.

Much is made of this tactic because business bankruptcy

courts are filled with those who rushed into some deal and made some ill-advised contract that could not be escaped by any other means.

When you are negotiating for a new job, make all of your agreements with the potential employer before you accept his offer. One top-flight marketing executive resigned his high paying job with a New York advertising agency to accept the marketing managership of a large wine merchandising organization. They picked his brains for a year and then cast him aside. He had no contract, not even a verbal understanding. He had just assumed that he would be treated with usual consideration. That assumption was unjustified in this case because the firm has the reputation of regularly doing just what it did to him.

Strike When It Hurts the Adversaries

Adversaries can be hurt at some times more than at others. If plans call for inflicting maximum damage on the foe, the timing of the plan should be such that it hurts him the most. While this tactic has far more application to the military than to business, it does have some industrial applications. One appliance manufacturer chose a time when a significant competitor's plant was on strike to launch a sales program designed to increase his number of distributors and dealers. He hoped that he would be able to take away those of the competitor's dealers who were unhappy at being unable to obtain supplies from the strike bound plant.

Joe, a golfer of modest skill, had a running battle with Bill, a more talented crony. The two foes had played together each Wednesday and Saturday for years, and over that time Joe had managed to win a considerable amount of money from the better player by a judicious timing of his bets. Joe had noted certain tendencies in Bill's game. On holes requiring tight drives, Bill was likely to slice rather badly as he eased up on his swing. Bill did very badly on two long par three's, so Joe would always try to get side bets down on those holes. Bill took the bait, because he was usually ahead at the time and felt obliged to do so. Often his whole game would disintegrate after blowing the bets on his weak holes.

Thus the wise manager takes care to hide his sensitive spots lest one's foes exploit them.

Don't Let Them Dig In

Speed is frequently essential in actions, to prevent the adversary from gaining a toehold or being able to solidify his position, thereby presenting a stronger counterforce at a later date.

When the Wilkinson Sword Company introduced its stainless steel double-edged shaving blade into the U.S. market a few years ago, the management of Gilette correctly saw that it would have to counter this move quickly to prevent Wilkinson from gaining a permanently large share of the market. Bon Ami, on the other hand, allowed Ajax and Glasswax to take away its markets with new products and aggressive advertising. It tried for three or four years to counterattack but failed miserably, thereby leading to the ultimate downfall of the company.

The major problem that must be guarded against in exercising this tactic is that in one's haste to strike he may devise a faulty plan. It is all too easy to rush off half-cocked to strike either at some undeserving problem or to strike improperly at the real problem.

One of Hitler's famous tactical blunders was to counter the

plans of General Rommel to meet the Allied armies on the beach and keep them from digging in and getting a foothold. Hitler kept his armor in reserve until long after the Allies were well established in their positions.

The owners of real estate have discovered to their dismay the price they pay for charitably allowing the public or someone to use their property. One resident of an oceanfront house generously allowed people to use her driveway to get to the beach. The land and the driveway were hers. The driveway was hers, that is, until some aggressive public official sued her in court to declare the driveway public domain because she had been allowing the public to use it. "By her action she admits that it is public property," were the words of the judge who listened to that nonsense. *Don't let them dig in!* Or even set foot on!

Grab It Now

A department head had to fill five openings in his organization under a severe handicap—a low wage scale. He happened to have the good fortune of being able to hire a certain man who was well recognized in the field but whose price was high. The manager went to his superiors to fight for the man and was given the choice: hire this man for his price and lower the salaries for the remaining four positions or forget this man. He grabbed the man. Later, he confided to a colleague, "That was a good stance they took, but they will come off of it when I bring the next person before them. Each time they will have to hire on the prospect's terms, because there is no way that we can fill the openings for the money they are offering. So I take what I can get now and worry about future problems when they come up."

Many investors are seemingly unaware of the discount mathematics of the present value of future funds which scream, "*Grab it now!* $1,000 now is worth $27,393, 20 years from now," when one takes into consideration a ten percent interest rate and an eight percent rate of inflation. Add to that a risk factor and the value of present funds is impressive.

Three men, partners in an industrial building, agreed to sell it on favorable terms to a buyer who did not have sufficient cash to swing the deal. Paper was offered in lieu of money. One partner was adamant about wanting his share in cash. The other two partners were so eager to sell that they agreed to take most of their share in paper—eight percent over ten years—a most unwise decision. That paper was hardly worth two-thirds of its face amount. Immediate cash should be demanded in most negotiations, unless there are tax considerations. Concessions can be given to get it.

A prime example of this principle is furnished by those well-publicized contracts given star athletes which defer payments well into the future. At the time of the signing management claims that it is paying millions, but it's mostly hot air. The athlete will be lucky to see much of it. Ask Spencer Haywood about the $3 million the Denver Rockets agreed to pay him—or so he and his lawyers thought. It didn't turn out that way. Of course, the tax laws are what entice people into such foolish deals.

When people promise to pay you money in the future, you may have trouble locating them when the time comes. And if they are available, they may not have the dough to pay off. Collection may be a long, costly process with scant chance of success. Grab the money as soon as you can. And don't be so afraid of the tax man that you make silly agreements to spite him.

5

Negotiating and Persuasive Tactics

One of the least discussed functions of the manager is that of negotiation. One of the surprises in store for the would-be top executive is the amount of time he will spend in negotiation; he will be negotiating constantly with somebody for something or other. He negotiates with bankers and investment brokers for money. He negotiates with labor unions over wage rates. He negotiates with the market over the price of his product. He negotiates with his subordinates over wages and other demands. He negotiates with suppliers for lower prices and landlords for lower rents. He negotiates with property owners for the sale of property. He negotiates with the government over taxes and other legal matters. Since the administrator constantly negotiates, his ultimate success almost completely depends upon his negotiating skills. The inept negotiator will always pay too much and get too little, thus being rendered competitively weak.

A manager is also continually trying to persuade someone to do something. This is the essence of implementing a plan. Once a plan has been formulated, the administrator must persuade, by one means or another, all parties necessary to the plan to carry out their parts of it. Persuasion can be a difficult task, for the parties may not always wish to cooperate.

Actually, you should realize that persuasion and negotiation are closely related tactical categories, for the essence of negotiation is to persuade the adversary to accept your terms.

While several of the tactics previously discussed are applicable to negotiating, the following ones seem more directly connected with the persuasive process.

It has been particularly encouraging to see several books published during the past few years on the art of negotiation. There is much good material in them which the ambitious businessman will find useful. In particular, we are beginning to understand better the true role of negotiating skill in one's career advancement. While we spend a great amount of time in sales training courses discussing all of the steps involved in the selling process, little time has been devoted to how to drive through to a deal. Putting together a deal is the essence of selling, the essence of business. Some people seem to have developed that skill admirably while others don't quite know how to do it. Far too many transactions slip by unfulfilled even though the prospect needed the goods and was interested in buying them. The salesman just did not know how to put the whole thing together.

Traditional salesmanship doctrine called this *closing*. The manager would declare that the person did not know how to close. But it is not that simple. There is more to it. Many skilled salesmen close repeatedly but do not know how to negotiate a deal. Much business does not fit the nice tidy model of someone buying a car or refrigerator right from the dealer's floor. The buyers have several barriers that must be hurdled before a deal is signed. Thus some tactics are necessary to get the job done.

Several common barriers are encountered in negotiations: money, trade-ins, services, and assurances. It has been said time and again that the art of negotiating lies in finding out what the other party wants and then showing him a way to get it while you get what you want. A good deal is one in which both parties get what they want. So, early in the process you will be trying to discover what it is that the other person really wants—not what he says he wants, but what he really wants. Experience clearly indicates that what people say they want and what they are really after are two different things. Sometimes the clever negotiator has to prove to the other party what they should really want. Some education must be done. This sounds high-handed and presumptuous, but it is reality.

Thus you might be facing an adversary who proclaims that the price is too high. Price seems to be barrier to the deal. Yet you sense that is not so. What the other party is really saying is, "I haven't got enough money to buy it." That is an entirely different matter and a much easier one to overcome. If you can work out some way for the other party to pay for the item, you can put together a deal.

Alice was the leading real estate saleswoman in a fairly large metropolitan area. In action she was a marvel to observe. A paragon of selling skills she wasn't. In fact, she hardly bothered trying to sell any of the properties. She would just show them and then ask, "Well, is this what you want?" When she found some property that the buyer liked, she went to work. She would put together the damndest deals depending upon the circumstances. First, she had an amazing knowledge of the money market. She knew where money was to be found and what its price would be. Furthermore, she knew the flexibility of contractural arrangements. There is no one way to sell something. A buyer and seller can agree on anything that makes sense to both of them. She knew how to give each party what it wanted.

Mike sold farm equipment in amazing quantities. His success was based on an uncanny knowledge of the market for used equipment. He could put together deals for new equipment because he knew how to get rid of the customer's old equipment at realistic prices. As he said, "I can't sell a farmer a new tractor until I can show him what to do with his old one. He isn't about to walk away from it." Thus many deals hang on the disposition of the existing equipment or property. This is particularly true of real estate.

There is also the limitless area of services and assurances which must be satisfactorily handled if the deal is to be made. Here believability is the key to the transaction. If the adversary does not believe what you say, what you put into writing, the deal is not likely to be consummated.

But let us get into some specific negotiating tactics.

Narrowing the Field

Early in negotiations one should endeavor to *narrow the areas of disagreement* between himself and the adversary so that there are disagreements on as few points as possible. In the early stages the parties should determine the areas in which they are in complete agreement and sign off those areas as agreed upon, leaving them closed thereafter. This is known as erecting roadblocks or barriers so that in later stages the adversary cannot come back and reopen these previously decided matters when he feels he is not getting his way in the areas of dispute. Once the field has been narrowed to as few points of dispute as possible, then negotiations can get underway on each point. It is advisable to focus negotiations on one point at a time, rather than wandering from point to point in confusion.

Evidently the negotiations between Dr. Kissinger and the North Vietnamese broke down at the end of 1972 when the North Vietnamese reneged on agreements that had been made earlier in negotiations, a breach of etiquette certain to blow negotiations out of the water. There is no way you can negotiate with people who continually change their minds, whose word cannot be relied upon. Such behavior is a certain sign that either the other party is really not interested in negotiating in good faith or that they are inept amateurs. In the first case, clear out; in the second instance, give them a quick course in the principles of negotiation.

Thus it can be seen that negotiations require a great deal of discipline. Complicated negotiations such as occur in labor relations and between nations not only require great physical and mental stamina but also a great deal of organization and structure. Much time is spent early in such negotiations in efforts to agree on the issues to be negotiated, their order of consideration, and the rules under which the negotiations will be conducted.

Step-by-Step

Perhaps this age-old tactic has been popularized most by Dr. Kissinger's effective use of it during negotiations in the Middle East. It serves in distinct contrast to the negotiating tactic of first agreeing in broad principle on a matter and then working out the details.

In *step-by-step* the negotiator focuses all attention on but one issue to get agreement on that matter before any other agenda item is discussed. Also notice how Kissinger used one-on-one in Middle East negotiations. It would have been impossible to get all the Arab powers around a table with Israel let alone pound out any sort of an agreement from such a meeting. It would have quickly turned into a shouting match in which each leader would have successfully tried to out do the previous speaker in appealing to his people. No good would have come of such a tactic. Rather Kissinger focused on Egypt first in the correct belief that Egypt had the best reasons for negotiating a peace agreement. If Egypt could be persuaded to sign a peace agreement, more pressure would automatically be placed upon the remaining Arab powers to come to terms. Moreover, certain precedents would have been established which would probably aid in future settlements.

Not only is step-by-step a negotiating tactic but it is also an operating tactic. In undertaking any large endeavor the administrator may be well advised to break it down into small concrete steps—take it one step at a time. Many adversaries shy away from accepting any large scale proposal but will agree to items one by one.

Jack accepted the presidency of a medium-sized machine tool manufacturing concern that was in serious trouble. He felt that he clearly saw what had to be done to turn the situation around. While there are many tacticians who would have advised Jack to make all his changes at one time in alignment with Machiavelli's advice on the matter, Jack felt that his situation called for a different tactic. He really did not want to lose many people but rather just change some of their ways. His whole program would have overwhelmed them and lead to charges that Jack was too grandiose in his aspirations. He decided to lay his program out before them slowly, one step at a time. It worked. Fortunately, Jack had sufficient time for the tactic to work for it does take patience and time to use step-by-step. It is not a tactic for an impatient person.

Step-by-step has several obvious virtues. First, it allows the administrator to focus attention on one matter at a time thus increasing the likelihood of a wise and successful decision on it. Second, it allows for adjustments in strategy and demands in later stages if things do not go as planned in the earlier ones. Each step can be adjusted depending upon what happened during the previous one. Third, it makes a large difficult negotiation seem practical whereas if one was to look at the whole picture one might consider the matter hopeless.

The Blank Check

The faculty of one business school felt a strong desire to change its curriculum rather radically. They felt that any change had to be for the better and the desire was so overwhelming that they finally decided to do something about it. Long experience had painfully proved the impossibility of getting two professors, let alone a whole faculty, to agree on anything so complex as an entire curriculum. Any committee recommendations brought before the faculty were so chopped up before being passed that the end result was always pitiful. So the faculty granted the curriculum committee a *blank check* beforehand. They passed a motion that the committee had the power to institute a new curriculum without coming to the faculty for approval. This was a most unusual and interesting tactic.

If you are assigned some delicate or controversial task and do not wish to waste your time doing something that will come to naught when brought before a higher authority, then try to get a blank check to execute your plan without further authority. If your power is sufficient, your stand should be: no blank check, no work! One cannot easily do this in most work situations, but the tactic is quite applicable in other affairs. A Little League board asks you to head up the umpires; get a blank check to run the operation as you see fit with no second guessing from the board. The time to get the blank check is before you undertake any task or job. Get the authority you need and want before accepting the job.

Let us hasten to admit that other people will seldom be willing to grant you a blank check, so the tactic is used infrequently. However, you only use it when you really mean it. You should be unwilling to undertake the endeavor unless given carte blanche. Remember, all bets are made on the first tee. This tactic is a variation of that tactic. You get your power before you launch your efforts.

Bait Your Hook

You can't catch fish with a bare hook. If you want to reel in a prize fish you must *bait your hook* with the proper enticement. The easiest way to get somebody to do something you want them to do is to make it worth their while. It is amazing to note the number of managers who do not seem to understand this basic principle of motivation. They frequently expect the other person to do something out of the kindness of his heart or just because he is ordered to do it. If you really want somebody to do something, make sure you give him a good reason for doing it. Such things as bonuses, pay raises, vacations, or something else the adversary wants (possibly continued employment) can all be used as effective bait.

A large building contractor was having a difficult time persuading the authorities to grant him some much-needed zoning variances. He gained his way by baiting the hook with a small land grant to the city for a long desired park in the area.

There are really no adverse aspects to the use of this tactic, except that at times one may put too much bait on the hook, thereby increasing the cost of the plan beyond acceptability.

Many administrative problems are the result of faulty reward systems. The way people are paid often does not provide them enough incentive for doing the things management wants them to do. Make no mistake, reward systems work. If you want a person to do something, make it worth his while to do it.

The public screams that school teachers and professors are not as dedicated to teaching as they are to other pursuits—writing, research, consulting, and administration. Yet clearly, few people have ever been really rewarded for being good teachers. Indeed, one fears for the individual whose sole devotion is to the classroom, because his job is likely to be in jeopardy. The real dollar rewards in teaching are to be found elsewhere.

The president of a large publishing company was very unhappy with the efforts of his college sales force. They weren't very good at selling books; but then what did he expect? They were not being paid to sell books. It mattered not one whit to the salesman's pay whether he sold one book or tons of them. They were being paid for putting in time. That was changed. The men were put on a commission—no sell, no pay. The bait tendered to the sales force to get them to accept the new reward system was the distinct probability of higher earnings from the new system.

A recruiter for high administrative positions in Washington wanted to attract a certain person of proven talent to a particularly important post, but could not do so. The person would have had to sacrifice far too much to take the job. He would have had to sell stock, take a pay cut, and lose a good job. It's an old story. There's got to be some bait somewhere.

You've simply got to give the other person a valid reason to do what it is that you want him to do. It is unrealistic to expect him to act without such potential rewards. *You must have some bait on your hook!*

Disguise True Desires

An age-old horsetrading tactic is to never let the seller know which horse it is that the buyer is interested in, because as soon as the seller finds out, the price on it will immediately go up. The adept buyer goes to great lengths to *disguise his true interests*. This means that the truly important negotiating factors may not come up first, but sometimes are brought in later as seemingly minor side issues. One young man, who was negotiating with a potential employer for a job, focused most of the negotiations on money to disguise the fact that he had already made up his mind to accept the job because he wanted to live in that particular community. Had his strong desire to live in that area been disclosed to the employer, the man's bargaining position for money would have been completely destroyed and he would have had to accept a much lower salary.

At times it may be wise to feign disinterest in a proposition at first, no matter how much you like it, because if you are too eager you may scare off the other party.

A businessman, because of his overeagerness to sell his sick business, repelled many potential buyers. If you are too eager in accepting an adversary's offer, he may quickly withdraw it because he assumes that he has been too generous. Always try to allow the other party to believe that he has made a good deal.

Be Your Own Casting Director

Sometimes people will play the role in which they are cast. If you wish them to play a particular role for you, you must *be the casting director*.

A salesman had been having a very difficult time cracking a particularly large industrial account, largely because of the obstinate behavior of a purchasing agent who strongly favored a competitor. The salesman approached the purchasing agent with the statement, "Sir, from what I have heard about you, you are a most impartial purchasing agent who firmly adheres to the proven policy of maintaining multiple sources of supply on critical items." He tried to cast the purchasing agent into the role he wished him to play.

This tactic is based largely on two psychological forces. First, the laws of suggestion come into play here, as many people will instinctively play the role which has been suggested for them. Second, many people are highly accommodating; they want the other person to like them and are constantly trying to perceive and play the role that is expected of them by the other party. One should never be afraid of playing the role of a casting director, because there is really little that can go wrong in applying this tactic if it is done with some finesse and does not run counter to the person's self-concepts.

An entrepreneur who was trying to sell his landscaping services to the branch manager of a large corporation's distribution center in Dallas approached the negotiations saying, "I can see by all your advertising and your plant that your company takes a lot of pride in itself and its products. You people really do a first class job with everything you touch. Isn't that right?"

The branch manager beamed as he admitted that the statement was true. Then the entrepreneur continued, "I would think that you would want the outside of your fine plant here to also look first-class at all times. Here is a picture of what it looks like now. Here's what some other plants that we maintain that are similar to this one look like. Don't you think that the home office would want you to have us put your grounds into first-class shape?"

He got the contract. He had cast the buyer in the role of a proud man.

Carry a Big Stick

Many staff people and assistants to some chief executives accomplish their persuasive ends in the names of their bosses—they *carry a big stick;* that is, they constantly carry with them the authority of their superiors. The subordinates or other executives whom they are attempting to persuade are tacitly threatened with having the assistant report back to his superior that the other party was uncooperative. Many times the staff person opens a conversation with such words as, "The boss would like me to . . . ."

A person who continually goes around overtly using the authority of his superior is certain to inspire feelings of antagonism from his subordinates. This type of individual is easily disliked and is ultimately bound to create disaster for himself. If a person has enough enemies in the organization, sooner or later they will get him. No one likes to have rank pulled on him, so while this tactic will work a few times, its use should be highly selective.

While it is generally true that if you really have power you do not have to flaunt it, there are times when your adversaries are unaware of your true power. In such encounters there are ways to communicate your power without overtly declaring it. Associates can proclaim it; certain status symbols may communicate it; or some indirect comment may be made that infers the possession of power. "I must meet one of my directors for lunch, so we'll have to break at noon."

There are situations in which the manager is doomed if he does not have a big stick or if he has one but is reluctant to use it. Some people understand only power. They run all over the person who cannot use power to control them. The examples from civil service situations are numerous and one case might be enlightening here. A man of considerable talent assumed the directorship of a governmental research unit that was notorious for the laxity and indifference of its people. Rather quickly he set about to gather evidence concerning the incompetence and malfeasance of people he observed goofing off. It took some time and effort but it had to be done. Then he brought charges against them and fought terrible battles with civil service boards; but he won all of his battles. His group got the message and went to work. He had to use a big stick to get their attention.

Bring Your Own Expert

Many times the manager lacks the expertise with which to establish himself as an authority on some matter at issue with an adversary. He thereby places himself at a distinct disadvantage in their persuasive maneuverings. In such cases, it is a sound tactic for one to *bring his own expert* with him to the confrontation, especially one whose credentials are distinctly superior to those of the adversary.

A newly hired sales manager of a large metals company was having a difficult time persuading the company's comptroller to change the firm's traditional method of paying the expenses of its salespeople. Previously the company had been paying its people one lump sum for both salary and expenses, thereby forcing the salespeople to differentiate between the two for the satisfaction of the Internal Revenue Service. The sales manager wished to pay them their expenses separately, so that they would be relieved of both a great deal of book work and difficulties with the income tax people. This was part of the plan he wished to institute for making the sales job easier, so that the sales force could devote more time to actually selling the company's products. The comptroller's reluctance to accommodate the sales manager was largely based on the inconvenience it was going to cause him in changing the company's system. To conceal the real reason for his reluctance he proposed some fallacious legal arguments in the hope of quickly bluffing the sales manager out of his plan.

The sales manager retained the services of a recognized expert in the field of compensation and expenses. The sales manager introduced the comptroller to his expert, citing all of the credentials and writings that clearly established him as an authority in the field. The meeting progressed into the matter of paying salesmen's expenses. For some strange reason, all the arguments the comptroller had previously been proposing seemed to evaporate in a short ten-minute session during which the sales manager was able to have his way on the matter. The comptroller put forth some legal defenses, only to be refuted by the expert, who cited the Revenue Code with a great deal of authority.

Many times an adversary will try to bluff you if he knows that you are uninformed in an area; his bluff is called if you have your own expert to examine his cards carefully.

Set Up Straw Men

An age-old negotiating tactic is to *set up straw men* for the adversary to knock down, thereby leading him to believe that he has won a victory. A straw man is some demand or condition that the manager puts forth solely for the opposition to knock down. He is not at all serious about the straw man and fully expects it to be annihilated, but he fully intends to extract his price for allowing the straw man's annihilation. The adept manager will frequently establish several straw men and, not too surprisingly, if he faces inept adversaries, he may receive some rewards he did not anticipate.

Typically, clever negotiators slowly probe and test every claim and demand made by their adversaries to see which are straw men and which are hard-core demands. Hence, the tough negotiator does not want to give all his straw men away too quickly, lest he be discovered and disarmed in the mental battle fought between negotiators.

Naturally, straw men must be logical and have some support or they may be brushed aside lightly by the adversaries, with no resulting gain for the administrator.

Clever husbands long ago learned the adept deployment of straw men. "Honey, the boys at the plant want me to go hunting with them in the Sierras." After his wife lodges her expected objections to the venture, the dutiful spouse petulantly resigns the cause implicitly, saying, "Okay, you win this time—but you owe me one!" The fact that he had no real desire to go up there and freeze to death with that bunch of drunkards must be carefully hidden. Since the rules of modern marriage imply that one must win and lose in some reasonable ratio, arrange to lose encounters that you don't want to win—that is, set up straw men.

Nose in the Tent or Foot in the Door

Another age-old tactic is for the manager to settle for small, immediate gains in certain areas hitherto impenetrable, in the hope that once he has his *nose in the tent* he will be able to move in slowly and take over more of the tent. The tactic works surprisingly well. Once a precedent is broken, it is much easier at a later date to negotiate even larger concessions. Small concessions often lead to larger ones.

Sometimes a consultant will undertake work for a promising client at a relatively attractive price and perform superbly in the hope that he can get his foot in the door or his nose in the tent. Sometimes a company will shave its price or offer special services in order to get a foot in the door of some large, potential account.

The basis of success for this tactic is that the first demand must seem so utterly reasonable that it cannot be turned down. Because the manager seems to want only a very small concession, the adversary is highly tempted to give it to him in the hope that he will be buying permanent peace by doing so. People tend to discount potential future trouble if they gain peace in the present.

In the proxy battle for control of MGM several years ago, the outsiders who were endeavoring to ascend to management first approached MGM's president with the proposition that they would be content if they were given only two seats on the board of directors. The president was a modest man who also considered himself to be fair. He also prized a peaceful existence. The outsiders represented a substantial holding of stock, so he concluded that for sake of his peace of mind it would be sensible to give them two seats on the board. Once on the board, the two outsiders used their position to cause such an unimaginable legal mess that the president eventually lost his job. It is unwise to let your foes inside where they can learn things that can be used against you. Information is quite important in such struggles.

Leave the Lid on Pandora's Box

There are many occasions in the negotiations between people when one is tempted to introduce a new subject or reopen one that has been closed. This is an exceedingly dangerous undertaking and should only be done after it has been given much thought.

If you decide to open up a new area—*take the lid off Pandora's box*—you can never be quite certain what will come out, as your adversary may take the opportunity to enlarge his demands or use the new topic as a springboard into some other area. The more factors that you bring into a negotiation, the more difficult you make it. One of the basic tactics in bargaining is to narrow the scope or number of issues involved in the bargaining, and opening up "Pandora's box" counters that sound tactic.

In its purest form, this tactic means that the manager should be extremely wary of venturing into areas that good judgment tells him are fraught with potential troubles. A small manufacturer was increasingly disenchanted with the agents who were selling his wares to gift stores throughout the nation. He thought that they were not very good at it, so he fired them and hired ten men of his own. Once he had lifted the lid on Pandora's box he paid dearly for everything that came out—expense accounts, sales management problems, and resistence to his line by former dealers who were under the influence of the firm's former agents.

Opening up a Pandora's box is the sign of a poor manager who is unable to anticipate the potential results of his managerial actions.

The inexperienced manager is most likely to fall into this trap, because he has yet to learn how interconnected everything in his operating system can be. When something is changed in one part of the system, its impact will be felt in many places throughout the system. The wise manager foresees those impacts and either is prepared to accept them or has made arrangements to deal with the new problems.

M.B.A. students studying business policy are particularly prone to making this tactical error in their case analyses. They will rashly propose to do one thing or another without being prepared to deal with the results of that action. It is very difficult to get them to foresee the results of their recommendations and to have plans ready to deal with those outcomes.

Shoot for the Moon

A standard negotiating tactic is to *ask for the moon* and settle for less, so that the other party feels he won some sort of victory. Labor union leaders have long used this tactic in their negotiating sessions with management, correctly surmising that if they shoot for the moon they have nothing to lose.

However, in more realistic managerial situations there are some dangers in employing this tactic, because the manager who is overly dependent upon it will have his demands completely discounted by his adversaries as he becomes known as a moon shooter.

A young manager, who had been offered a particularly challenging job loaded with problems, made many demands upon management as a condition of his accepting the responsibility. He included in his demands just about everything imaginable that he could possibly need to deal with the problems. While he knew perfectly well that he would not be granted all of his demands, he still made them in the hope of getting as many of them as possible. Moreover, he wanted to have on record before accepting the job what he thought it would take to remedy the situation. If he failed in the task, he had created a possible scapegoat—his boss had not given him what he needed to be successful.

A dean addressed the chairman of his marketing department, "We have been given nine new positions for next year. As I see it, your department will only have to lose .75 of its 13.5 positions." The chairman protested, of course, that there was no basis for such a cut. The dean replied, "Well, my estimate is only tentative. We'll see what develops."

The next budgetary document distributed by the dean indicated that the marketing department would remain at 13.5 men.

All of this was designed by the dean to head off a departmental request for an additional person.

Had the department chairman been playing the dean's game, he would have originally asked for two more people and then settled for one. However, in this instance it was not a matter of concern for the chairman because he had another game going—to capitalize on the defeat. He wanted the dean to win the contest because it served his purpose.

Raise the Stakes—Buy the Pot

A well-recognized principle of poker is never to put your feet under the table with a man richer than yourself, because he will be able to seize pots that are legitimately yours by betting so heavily that your good sense forces you to fold. When you simply cannot afford to stay with him, he has *bought the pot.*

Large organizations lock smaller ones out of certain markets by making the stakes too high for the small ones to afford even to look at some cards in the game. A certain political organization was able to restrict the bidding for large paving contracts to a selected few contractors by making the bonding requirements so high that the smaller contractors could not play the game.

A large electronics manufacturing concern bidding for a sizable defense contract removed one troublesome smaller firm from the picture by an interesting combination of tactics, the essence of which was that the price of the game became too expensive for the smaller firm. Mr. Big approached Mr. Small with the proposition that if Mr. Small would not bid on the contract, and if Mr. Big got it, Mr. Small would be given a subcontract for a sizable section of the work. Moreover, no matter what might happen on the bid, Mr. Small would be given some subcontracting work on which the two concerns had been negotiating for some time. However, should Mr. Small decline this invitation to collude, Mr. Big would cut off all present subcontracts and investigate the possibility of a patent infringement suit on a matter of dispute between them in another affair. Whee! The price of poker had just gone up! Mr. Small could not afford to call Mr. Big's hand. If the antitrust implications bother you, don't worry, because this was an international incident.

On the other hand, a manager must be careful not to raise the stakes of a game so high that his friends and allies cannot play with him. One avid golfing executive had enjoyed excellent relations with several of his peers with whom he played golf weekly at a local municipal course. His fortunes increased suddenly so he joined a rather expensive country club, only to find out that his former friends could no longer stay with him. He was too expensive a playmate for them. Relations between the old friends were not quite the same thereafter.

Learn the Adversary's Limits

The key to successful negotiating is to *learn the limits of the other party;* that is, the extent beyond which he will not go. Once the adversary's limits are learned, negotiations become relatively easy; one knows just how far the adversary can be pushed before negotiations will be severed. Once a purchasing agent learns that a salesman will lower his price to a given level, that is exactly where the bargaining will end up. Conversely, once a salesman learns that a purchasing agent will pay so much, that is what the price will be.

It is most important for the negotiator not only to conceal his own limits, but also to disguise or even mislead the adversary as to exactly what those limits are. Used-car salesmen frequently ask the potential buyer what he wants for his old car. It is a mistake to disclose one's price first. Obviously, the seller is at a distinct disadvantage in most situations because he is required by tradition to quote a price first, which forms the upper limit from which bargaining takes place. Astute horsetraders try to get would-be purchasers to bid before quoting a price in the hope that the bid will be higher than the intended asking price.

A good deal of the time the seller's lower limits are set by what he can get for his goods elsewhere. If he can make the buyer believe that he has a bona fide offer in his pocket for a certain desired amount, it will force the buyer to either forget about the deal or better the offer. A homeowner trying to sell his own home was in an extremely weak bargaining position due to his particular circumstances, but he had to have at least $45,000 for his house. He kept an official looking offer from a fictitious buyer handy so that prospective buyers could "accidentally" see it on his desk as they wandered through the house. As the house was well worth the money, he was able to set his lower limits rather effectively. He sold the house for $45,500.

The seller's costs are certainly one factor affecting his limits. People do not sell below cost unless they are forced to do so; thus if the buyer can gain access to the seller's costs, he has a bargaining advantage. Several services now provide such information to auto buyers for use in bargaining with car dealers.

On the other side, the seller would like to know how much money the buyer can pay. Available cash may be a limitation, his credit another. The buyer's real alternatives are most critical.

Really, this matter of bargaining rests on the managing of limits—make the other party believe your stated limits and discover his actual ones.

Run a Bluff

Bluffing is the essence of negotiation and bargaining. Bluffing is the art of making one's adversary believe something that makes him do what the bluffer wants him to do when the adversary, if previously unconvinced, would most likely have acted to the disadvantage of the bluffer. The bluff may entail making the adversary think that one has other buyers willing to pay more for something, or it may entail leading one's superior to think that other companies are trying to lure him away.

Running a bluff is an art in itself. It requires several of the tactics discussed here, plus an ability to act convincingly and behave persuasively. The good bluffer is a con man; he makes people believe things that aren't so.

There are situations in which it is unwise to run a bluff, because it may be called. One successful football coach made demands for more money after each successful season; his bluff consisted of pressuring the board of trustees with the threat of leaving the university for a pro coaching job. Actually, the man had little desire to go into pro ranks. He was well situated in his position and his family was quite happy there. After pulling this holdup game three years in a row, the board of trustees finally handed him his hat and said, "It's been nice knowing you!" They called his bluff. The coach had no alternative but to accept the pro job, one that he was not particularly happy with. From that point on the story was not very pretty.

There are times when the manager is ill-advised to bluff unless he is prepared to accept the consequences of having his bluff called, because that will happen in most instances. So don't bluff in situations where you can't afford to have the bluff called.

Bluffs are most effective when supported by some visual evidence. In a five-card stud game, four spades showing certainly makes for good bluffing material. The same type of evidence is needed to support other bluffs. A young junior executive (whatever that is) wanted more money and more responsibility, but he was hampered in his search for success by the fact that he liked his job, his boss, and did not really want to leave. Moreover, he had good reason to believe that his boss liked him and wanted to keep him, but something had to be done to precipitate some action towards his advancement. After reading *The Organization Man*, in which Whyte presented the correct philosophy that the only way one can really get a raise is through a tacit threat to go elsewhere for employment, he developed a bluff supported by that bit of information. At an opportune time he asked his boss for advice on a business proposition that had allegedly been made to him that would have resulted in his having to change employers. He thus indirectly placed the superior on notice that unless some benefits were forthcoming shortly, he might go elsewhere for them.

Most importantly, never bluff unless you are willing to live with the results of having that bluff called. The chances are that most bluffs will be called. Expect it! The bluff is a percentage play in which the player is willing to pay the price of having the bluff called; he hopes that he will benefit later by having introduced to the adversary's mind the idea that the player is a bluffer. That thought can be expensive to the adversary when the player really holds the winning cards at a later time. In business that exact situation is not common. Usually it is not wise to lead one's business adversaries to believe that he is a bluffer. Rather it is more to one's advantage to be known as someone who tells it straight. Here we see the difference between good card playing and good business.

Keep a Trump Card

In serious negotiations it is highly advantageous to *have a trump card* to play if needed. One might prefer not to play it unless forced to do so, but at least he should have it to win the game if he feels it is important to do so.

A minority stockholder of a small corporation was attempting to get a fair price for his stock in a squeeze-out maneuver being put on him by the majority stockholders. The majority stockholders were trying to cheat him in the deal. The minority stockholder's trump card was that the majority stockholders had been guilty of many illegal practices, including cheating on their income taxes, and the minority stockholder knew where all the bodies were buried. This was the trump card that he hoped that he would not have to play, but if they did not negotiate a fair settlement, he was fully prepared to file suit against them for misuse of corporate assets. However, he had to be very careful not to overtly threaten them with such suits because there are laws dealing with such threats.

Trump cards can be held secretly and brought out into the open only when needed in the last moments of battle.

There are really no drawbacks to the holding of trump cards. It is just a matter of knowing when—and if—they should be played. Of course the manager is never quite certain of what trumps the adversaries hold and whether or not they are higher ones.

The Documented Lie

One basic tactic in negotiating is *the documented lie*. Purchasing agents have been known to falsify documents to demonstrate the low prices of competitors for the purpose of getting a supplier to lower his price. The negotiator can prepare all sorts of cost figures and work up substantial documentation to prove that he must get a certain price for his product. Real estate agents have been known to put a larger amount of federal transfer stamps on deeds in order to make future buyers believe that a property sold for a higher price than was actually negotiated.

The purpose of this tactic is to mislead the adversary about your limits. People tend to accept the other fellow's costs as a lower limit since it is fairly well accepted that few people are willing to sell things below cost. So an art of documenting costs has come to the fore in bargaining situations.

As a general rule, people have been trained to believe things that are in writing without questioning their authenticity. Some negotiators, therefore, arrange to have proper documentation for their statements deliberately shown to the adversary, or the adversary may be allowed to sneak a look at the documents at an opportune time. Purchasing agents have been known to leave their offices deliberately to allow a salesman to sneak a look at competitive bids on a desk.

On the humorous side, a southern California golfer was visiting another golfing friend in Oregon who had lined up a match with two of the local hustlers who carried handicaps of two and three respectively. Prior to the match, the Oregonian golfer had his visitor type on a slip of paper, "This is to certify that Mr. southern Californian has a SCGA handicap of ten (10). (Signed) Manny 'One Putt' Hawkins, PGA, Little Gulch Country Club."

"But ten *is* my handicap," protested the visitor.

"I know, but believe me, these thieves won't believe a word of it. It's got to be on paper!"

Both "2" and "3" carefully inspected the document before grudgingly giving the man his ten blows. I'll not disclose the final financial outcome of this nonsense; I only advise all 10-

handicaps to leave 2's and 3's alone. No good will come of such a match.

Care should be taken not to be caught presenting false documentation to people with whom you must have future dealings, for this will destroy your effectiveness with them.

This tactic seems to be a favorite among the international fun-and-games tricksters—espionage agents. In World War II Hitler was misled about the exact location of the invasion of Europe by a cleverly planted set of documents which his agents were allowed to intercept. The Allies sold him a lie based on false documents.

The Red Herring

In both negotiating and persuading, sometimes the adroit manager must drag a red herring across the path of the adversary in order to confuse him or divert his attention.

The red herring tactic has defensive overtones, because it is most frequently used in giving false justifications for certain actions when the manager does not care to reveal the true ones. In many instances it is not wise to reveal the real reasons for undertaking an action. One is often best advised to draw a red herring across the path by giving false—but socially acceptable and rational—reasons for the action.

The sales manager ordered a salesman to move from his territory in eastern Pennsylvania to one in Nebraska "in order to bolster up the weak Nebraska territory." The salesman resigned, as the manager had expected him to do, for he knew the man had deep roots in Pennsylvania. The real reason underlying the sales manager's actions was that the man had been a troublemaker and the sales manager wished to get rid of him. It would not do for the real reason to be exposed; a red herring was in order.

A company's executive committee was discussing the advisability of hiring a certain man as comptroller. All evidence indicated he was an outstanding candidate for the job. All but one member on the committee were in favor of making the man an offer. The dissenter then offered a red herring: "Before we act, I think we should have a study made to see whether or not we should split that job up into two positions." The others were onto the dissenter's tactics, because he was always making such diversionary plays, so they ignored his red herring and voted to extend the offer.

Properly executed, the red herring tactic is a fairly safe tactic. Even if the adversaries suspect its existence, there is little they can do except have their suspicions.

Military affairs have traditionally made great use of the art of misdirection. Able leaders continually endeavor to make the opponents think the wrong things by dragging a red herring across their trail. Eisenhower had Patton create a false army and parade around a certain location in England to encourage the Germans to think that the invasion would take place at Calais. Patton was the red herring.

Be Unreasonable

One expert wrote an article in *Harvard Business Review* that the art of being a good negotiator rested on being completely unreasonable. His theory was that *good negotiators are unreasonable* and are able to force unreasonable demands on people who are intimidated by such unreasonableness. Weaker negotiators fail and fall by the wayside. Many labor union leaders use this tactic, sometimes bulldozing their way to better settlements for the membership than would have been possible had they taken a "fair and reasonable" approach.

The use of this tactic can be easily observed in world politics as certain foreign nations take a completely intractable and unreasonable stand for a long period of time until the adversaries are thoroughly convinced that nothing can be done with them. Then and only then do they back down sufficiently that an agreement can be reached. The adversaries in these cases are frequently so happy to get any concessions at all from a situation that was considered completely hopeless that they will grab at a deal that they would have dismissed previously.

Some sharp real estate investors use this tactic in buying their properties. They make a ridiculously low offer to a seller in the hope that some unknown circumstance will force the owner to accept it. In any event, it sets a low base from which to negotiate.

The only risk involved in such tactics is that the seller might become angry and refuse to even come to the bargaining table because he believes it would be a waste of his time.

This tactic cannot be used to negotiate with people with whom the manager must continue on a friendly, social basis. It is not recommended as a way of making friends. It is strictly a hard-headed negotiating tactic to be used in a few circumstances.

Keep Talking

One of the fundamental tactics in all negotiations is to *keep talking*, no matter how far apart you might be from agreement with the adversary. One can see the application of this in the peace councils of the world in which the adversaries, no matter how antagonistic and far apart their stands may be, still force themselves to come back to the bargaining table week after week to keep talking. As long as people are talking, there is little likelihood of fighting. It seldom pays to sever communications with your adversary if you are trying to bargain with him. This is akin to keeping the door open. Frequently, if one keeps talking with an adversary, some basis of a compromise can be worked out or some accommodation can be developed.

There are a few instances in which continued talking may be a disservice to the negotiator. The personalities of some adversaries are such that they disdain talking and view with contempt people who do so; in such situations, the less said the better. If the negotiator is taking a firm and reasonable stand on something, continued talks may indicate a willingness to compromise. To avoid giving this impression, the manager may have to cease negotiations.

One danger in talking so much during negotiations is that one may disclose things during the discourse that would preferably have remained secret. One big advantage to a negotiator in encouraging the adversary to talk is that he may learn some valuable information that will give him the upper hand.

Once the adversary senses that the talking stage of a confrontation is over, that he cannot gain his ends by talking, then he must either resort to other devices or fold his tent. Thus the cessation of talking can signal the instigation of stronger actions.

Keep Quiet

Silence is certainly a tactic, many times a most worthy one. When you talk you either say nothing, making you appear the fool, or you say something, giving away intelligence that may be used against you. In either case, nothing is gained. The wise manager only imparts intelligence that he wants to give out. This tactic is particularly important when negotiating with an adversary who is talkative. If the other party wants to talk, let him. The more he talks the more you may learn. In any event, the adversary is not learning a whole lot. As a general rule, you can always judge who has the upper hand in negotiations by observing who is doing the talking and who is doing the listening. The listener is usually holding the upper hand. The talker is trying to persuade him to come his way. Thus if you can maintain the aura of silence, you may project the image that you feel you are holding the upper hand even when such might not be the case.

The problem with giving an immediate reaction to some proposal is that it is quite likely that you will be making a mistake in doing so. Many times there are unseen factors in the picture that will only be perceived after considerable thought and analysis is made of the proposal. While it may seem to you on the spur of the moment that the adversary's proposal is quite agreeable, there may be some booby traps in it; thus it is frequently wise to say little other than, "We must first give it a thorough analysis."

As is true of many tactics, this one can backfire. In some negotiations you must be prepared to act quickly and with some boldness. The person who stalls and is silent may be left waiting. There is a place for silence and there is a place for straight talking and the adept manager learns which is which.

Stall

Time is frequently an important factor in the final outcome of a negotiation. The time demands on each party may vary; one must reach an agreement before the other. If that is the case, then once a negotiator discovers that the time pressure on his adversary is greater than that on his side, he can *stall* the negotiations until the adversary must capitulate because of time. The tactics for stalling are many: plain delay, playing ill, being unable to attend meetings because of other meetings, and all sorts of other stalls that can make days turn into weeks and weeks turn into months, thereby placing greater and greater pressure on the adversary.

One young man used the stall to good advantage in attempting to gain a pay raise from a miserly employer. His superior wanted to know if the young man was going back to graduate school or not; the young man said that he hadn't made up his mind yet and it would depend upon a lot of factors yet to be decided. Periodically the superior would nudge the young man for his decision, but each time he would be stalled. Finally, he made the offer, "If you will tell me today that you will stay for another year, I'll give you an additional $1,000 a year raise." The subordinate accepted the offer. In a similar situation a superior could admittedly become angered and dismiss the man outright or demand that a decision be made; but in this particular instance the subordinate had sized up his superior correctly and knew that he was under pressure since a replacement would be difficult to locate.

Sometimes stalls can cover a period of years, during which the manager simply hopes to outlive the adversary. Sometimes in legal battles a stall can be most advantageous. Witnesses can move away, memories can be dimmed, and all sorts of events can take place over a length of time that may strengthen one's hand in a legal conflict if he is the defendant. Time is usually of the essence to the plaintiff.

Capitalize on Defeat

Into the life of every manager some rain must fall. He will lose on some issues. However, the adept loser *capitalizes on defeat* by extracting something from the winner as a consolation prize. Winners tend to be generous because of their natural psychological exuberance over winning, and are quite likely to grant some concessions if the loser takes his defeat gracefully.

A sales manager wanted to hire seven new people for better coverage of the marketing area, but he was flatly turned down by top management. However, in his defeat he was able to wring from management some much needed concessions for more liberalized expense accounts, something he had been trying to do for five years.

During one unfortunate year the dean of a large school of business administration lost a large number of his faculty members to other schools. As it happened, each of the professors left for various personal reasons and most of them did not improve themselves financially in their moves. However, the dean was able to use these resignations as a strong lever to gain some liberal salary increases for his remaining faculty. He presented the resignations to the administration, claiming that the people left for higher-paying jobs.

The key to capitalizing on defeat is for the vanquished to control his behavior carefully so that the winner will feel obligated to bestow some consolation. Should one kick up a fuss over his defeat, it would be easy for the victor to rationalize his not giving any concessions.

Sometimes a truly astute manager will offer a token battle in some matter he cares nothing about, not for the purpose of actually winning that battle, but for what he can really get from it in defeat. It can be a psychologically advantageous position if one is owed some consolation prize. However, this can be dangerous if overdone, because the manager can look ridiculous if he automatically opposes any plan action put forth. Sometimes a straight log-rolling approach will work better: "Oh, I'll give you what you want if you'll give me. . . ."

In the military world perhaps the German concept of the mobile, flexible retreat is a case in point. In retiring from the scene of a defeat the German army would extract a frightful toll on the victorious oncoming army by putting up short but vigorous fights from previously prepared, well-fortified positions. The German high command wanted to employ this tactic in the retreat from Russia hoping to cause so many Russian casualties that victory could evolve from defeat. However, Hitler ordered the German army to stand fast and not give up territory. Hitler's tactics in defeat were horrible. He seemed to have a mastery of offensive tactics but lacked an understanding of defense. He did not understand his commander's desires to "sell" the Russians real estate at a frightful price while keeping the German armies intact.

In the political arena, it has not been unknown for candidates who sensed they had little chance to win a nomination, or even an election, to withdraw in favor of the likely winner after negotiating some sort of deal with him. Winners can be generous; they can afford to be.

Waltz Them to the Courthouse Steps

In some negotiations in which there are legal disputes, one must be prepared to take his adversaries *right up to the courthouse steps* and possibly into the courtroom if he is to get justice. Many foes simply refuse to negotiate realistically until they are brought into court; the average person has a great aversion to going to court because of the costs, nuisance, and mental anguish involved in doing so. Consequently, many people will settle for far short of what they could legitimately claim just to stay out of court. People knowing this will seldom settle up until they are faced with the courtroom and the realities of all its ramifications. Hence, the manager in such cases should not dawdle around negotiating, but should file suit and take the adversary right up to the courthouse steps and negotiate from a stronger position.

On the other hand, when one is being sued by an adversary, he must be prepared to go right into court and not offer a settlement until both parties are on the courthouse steps. The adversary is more likely to be willing to compromise advantageously at that time than earlier when he thinks he holds all the cards. A person who is afraid of going into court is at a distinct disadvantage in legal negotiations; a great many negotiations come down to simply who is right or wrong legally.

Obviously, if one has a strong legal position his bargaining power is much greater than it would be otherwise; but one should not jump to the conclusion that a weak legal position robs him of all bargaining power. If the adversary has the strongest case imaginable, not having to go to court to collect it is of some value, and the only way you can get that value is by making him believe that he will have to go to court to get what he is justly owed.

A clothing merchant's delight with his new store was somewhat dimmed when the adjacent property owner informed him that six inches of the building was over the property line. A survey confirmed that it was so. The neighbor wanted $2,000 damages, but the merchant said no and refused to admit any liability at all. Finally the neighbor filed suit for $30,000; then the merchant settled for $4,000 on the advice of his lawyer. Some people just won't listen to anything but a court order, or the threat of one.

The new owner of an industrial property was warned by the previous owner that the tenant had a bad habit of not paying his rent on time or even close to it. "If you want your rent on time, you'll have to tack a three-day notice on his door!" And so it was. The new owner had to shake the rent out of the tenant each month. The kicker, in this case, was that the tenant was wealthy. He just had the idea that he should not pay anyone until he had to do so; he thought he was being clever.

On the other hand, the person who is unwilling to risk court will pay for his reluctance. While the following case is a bit complicated, such deals as this usually are. Bill was a C.P.A. who knew a good value when he saw one, so when his wife came home one evening excited about a house she had been shown by a realtor he had to go see for himself. Sure enough, it was an attractive property. But Bill had a good house and was not all that eager to suffer the agonies of moving, so he threw a low ball; he guessed that the house was worth about $150,000 so he offered $100,000, subject to the contingency that Bill sell the house he was living in first. However, the seller had the right to continue seeking another deal. If one were found, Bill had three days in which to complete the contract. In effect, Bill had procured a first refusal to buy in exchange for his modest earnest money deposit. The seller did go on trying to sell his property and finally found a buyer who offered $120,000. Naturally, the seller wanted the $120,000 deal in preference to Bill's $100,000 offer. It so happened that the $120,000 offer was obtained by a salesman working from the same office as the salesman who was handling Bill's deal, so Bill learned of the development rather quickly. Upon learning of the new development he rushed to the county recorder's office to record his contract to buy, then called the Title Insurance Company that was acting as escrow on the new $120,000 contract. He said, "Hey, you had better check with the recorder because you've missed the contract I have on that property. You go ahead and close and you're going to be looking at me." The deal fell out of escrow because the title company wanted no part of a potential lawsuit. Now the homeowner was furious; he was out $20,000 and he desperately needed it because he was in much financial trouble with his business. He ran for his lawyer's office only to learn that the deal was tight. Bill had the money ready and waiting to satisfy his end of the deal; he was ready to close. But the seller refused to do so. He would not sign although a series of lawyers all told him the same thing—he did not have a leg to stand on in court. Finally he folded and sold the property.

What he did not know was that had he taken Bill to the courthouse steps he would have been there alone. Bill did not want any part of such a lawsuit. He was bluffing. But the only way for the seller to find that out was to go to court. One can always settle as the judge walks into the room.

The Grapevine

Sometimes the wise manager persuades his target indirectly by sending him messages informally via *the grapevine.* An office manager was distressed by the tardiness and overly long coffee breaks that were being taken by his office staff. The situation had been degenerating for some time, with people dragging in later and later and taking longer and longer coffee breaks. He hesitated to make an issue of the matter, for fear of appearing to be a dictator. Nevertheless, he wanted to bring the practices under control. He asked his secretary to start the word along the grapevine that the people in the office should be more diligent about their work habits if they did not want them to be officially regulated.

The grapevine is a handy system to use when the manager wants to pass down messages that are better not made into formal orders. One of its advantages is that if it does not work, the formal order can come later with the manager reaping little disadvantage from having first tried the grapevine.

Take a Vote

If the manager is confident that he has the majority of his people behind him on a plan, he can pretend to have a certain degree of neutrality and propose that a vote should be taken to decide what should be done on the matter. One of the advantages of being the boss is that one can choose when or when not to *take a vote* on an issue. The wise manager does not take votes on matters where he knows he is going to be defeated. He will avoid, at all costs, votes on such issues because this lessens his prestige considerably.

There are certain dangers in submitting an issue to a vote, for there is always the chance that a meeting can run away from the manager. For one reason or another, the results of the vote might not be acceptable to him and might thereby pose a sticky problem.

The president of a conglomerate had been perplexed over what to do about a cable television system the company owned in a small town in the West. He and his vice-president strongly wished to keep it, in spite of its consistent cash losses and the fact that it had no hope for profitable operation in the future. Since some cable TV companies had made proposals to buy it, the president thought he would allow his board of directors to vote on the matter. He was confident that he could persuade the board to turn down the proposals; however, for the first time in the history of the firm, his board of directors overrode him and voted to sell. As an interesting sidelight, the president managed to cool the negotiations with the cable company as a stalling device in the hope that he could salvage the cable operation. At a board meeting one year later, the board again instructed the president to sell off the subsidiary, which he was finally forced to do. Since that time, the president has been very reluctant to submit anything to a vote of the board if he is in any way fearful of their decision. He only submits things that he has tested ahead of time with the individual directors so that he will not be surprised again.

Force the Issue

Sometimes there is no persuading the other party because he is adamant in the matter and no amount of persuasion will change his opinion. In such cases, managers have been known to *force the issue.* A top-notch salesman whose territory was in Texas was quite unhappy over being discriminated against by the home office. While management furnished cars to its men, they were economy models devoid of such things as air conditioning. The salesman felt that air conditioning was an essential accessory in his territory and he had been trying to persuade his manager of this need for several years without success. With the advent of the first 100-degree day of the year, the salesman sent a telegram to his manager that he was not going to work on any day that the temperature was over 90 degrees until he was provided with an air-conditioned car. This forced the issue: either give the man an air-conditioned car, fire him, or accept the layoff because of heat. The man won because he was an outstanding salesman and could not be replaced easily.

This tactic is obviously dangerous because most people strongly resent being forced to do anything against their will. It can only be used when the tactician is in a very strong position or if he does not care about the consequences of losing on the tactic. People frequently hand in their resignations to force an issue.

Listen

One of the soundest, least-used tactics in negotiation is careful, attentive *listening;* that is, listening to the other person to detect exactly what it is that he wants and exactly where he stands. Careful listening frequently discloses a great many things. The adversary's tone of voice and method of delivery frequently disclose his true motivation and feelings. Bluffs can be detected, lies discovered, if one will but listen.

The nice thing about listening as a tactic is that it entails no dangers. It is completely safe to use and one gives away nothing to boot.

Listening is much broader than just paying attention to what people say to you. It also encompasses what they don't say, what they leave out. This discloses what they don't want you to know and chances are that is precisely what you do want to know.

Pay particular attention to just how the other person words his statements to you. Clever liars are able to deceive and not be brought to account for their deceptions if discovered. They technically tell the truth in the words actually spoken, but effectively communicate a lie by leading you to believe something else. A partner kept telling his associate, "We have nothing to worry about!" in regard to a particular business deal that seemed to be in trouble. Well, when the roof caved in, he was right; they had nothing to worry about. They had lost their money, but it had been gone a long time before. Watch out for people who talk in generalities while you want specifics—they are evading the issue. Pin them down!

A great deal of money has been made, or saved, by a word overheard here or there. Go where the spirits flow; that's the garden where the indiscreet word grows.

A director of a small chemical company found himself sitting next to a thirsty sales manager of a competing company on a long, cross-country flight. The director was also an investment counselor and had introduced himself as such. The sales manager spoke at great length about what he was doing, about company plans, about many valuable things. The director learned a great deal that afternoon that was converted into money shortly thereafter.

Make Them Think They've Won

The manager is indeed clever who can win a victory, yet *make the vanquished feel they have won*. This is not as difficult as it might seem, for many times the two parties are fighting for different goals. Even in negotiations, where the manager has the best of the compromise, the vanquished can feel they have the best of the bargain. This tactic can work because many times the other party does not know the real basis against which to compare a victory or loss. A union leader may feel that he won a victory in getting a 15 cent per hour raise for his workers and the employer can let him feel that way; but the employer may feel that he has won the victory because he thought he was going to have to pay 25 cents and was prepared to do so. Automobile dealers are masters at this game; they always try to make a customer feel that he got a bargain price on his new car.

There are few dangers in using this tactic because everyone likes to believe he is a winner, whether or not down deep he really is convinced of this or not. It is most important that he is at least able to have the appearance of being a victor.

Clever managers in instituting some new plan or program stress to those people who are adversely affected by it how that program will benefit them. Accentuate the positive, eliminate the negative, the old song goes. Show them how they are winners under the new program. While it might be difficult to understand why such a tactic would work on anyone with half a mind, remember that people constantly search for rationalizations for the things that they do. A worker faced with doing something he does not approve of or which adversely affects him is posed a difficult problem. Either he must find some way to live with the new order in dignity or he must resist. To resist poses risks, risks that most people don't care to take because their jobs would be jeopardized. Thus when shown how they win under the new program, they want to believe it because it make their life easier. Always remember, the other person wants to win, or if he loses at least he wants to think he won. If the first cannot be his, he will settle for the latter.

Avoid Personalities

Avoid, at all costs, dealing in personalities. Instead, focus your arguments around the facts of a case. Never call the adversary names, attack him personally, or question his honesty and sincerity, even though you may be severely provoked to do so. Such attacks only arouse emotional antagonisms. No matter how unscrupulous or questionable the adversary's tactics may be, it is probably advisable to avoid commenting directly about his personality.

A disappointed subordinate confronted his boss in the office one day to ask for a raise. When his overtures were spurned, he accused the superior of breaking his word and blamed him personally for his own lack of advancement. This was a serious blunder, no matter how true it might have been, because no one likes to be called a liar. Wise people seek to blame other forces outside the executive's control. He might reply to the superior, "I realize that you would like to give me this additional money if you could, but that the conditions of this company are such that it is impossible at this time. Could you tell me exactly what it is that is holding up my advancement and when might I expect it?" Personal attacks usually sever communications and can permanently alienate the parties to such a degree that relations become impossible.

Always focus negotiations on the facts and the issues that are involved in the particular situation. Be assured that personal attacks on adversaries make negotiations even more difficult, perhaps even impossible.

In daily dealings with one's associates it is easy to slip into personal references, sometimes seriously and sometimes only in jest. Regardless, the other people are not amused. A young man of great promise was blocked in his advancement because he had irritated his colleagues by a bad habit he had developed in meeting people. Everytime he greeted another person he opened up the conversation with some put-down based on the other person's characteristics. One of his colleagues was of Polish descent, so most conversations with that person were opened by saying, "How's our token Polack today?" or some equally crude comment. He frequently greeted one of his overweight colleagues with a comment about the man's paunch.

And so it went. No one was spared. No matter how innocent, it just does not pay to become too personal because you never know how sensitive the other party is.

Plant the Seed

In dealing with some types of people, the manager must be quite unobtrusive in trying to persuade them to do something. In such circumstances, he frequently is able to reach his desired ends by merely *planting a seed* in the mind of the right party. Suggestion is a potent persuasive tactic. Sometimes an entire plan can be suggested by merely planting a seed of thought in the mind of the right individual.

The president of a large electronics company wanted to discontinue a huge Christmas party that the company had given annually to its employees; the affair had become unmanageable over the years. Because of depressed conditions in the industry, the company had to lay off a large number of production workers during the month of October. In a "chance" meeting with the shop steward, the president casually voiced concern over the plight of the laid off people, with Christmas coming up and all. In an apparently offhand manner, he commented that he felt rather guilty about the company spending money on the Christmas party when all of the laid off people were having a hard time of it. He casually said, "It's too bad we can't give them the money instead of drinking it up!" The seed was planted and it grew. Within the week there was a formal request by the union that the money the company normally spent on the Christmas party be divided among the laid off workers. The president commended the union on coming up with such a noble idea.

This is an exceedingly sound tactic to use as frequently as

possible; it achieves maximum persuasive impact because the adversary thinks the idea was his. When he proposes it, you make him look good by complimenting him on his wisdom and judgment. There is little to be lost by trying this tactic; if it doesn't work something else can be tried later. It's major disadvantage is that it may take time to execute and the precise plan the other person may come up with might not be exactly what the manager had in mind.

Where the Body's Buried—Blackmail

It has not been unknown for managers to use *blackmail* to achieve their goals; the foundations of this tactic rest in knowing where the adversary has buried his bodies. Of course, this can be an exceedingly dangerous tactic to use, unless one is quite certain of his facts and the hold they will have over the adversary, because few people approve of blackmail. The most effective use of this tactic is in just knowing where the body's buried, but not overtly using this knowledge for blackmail purposes. The secretary who knows the peculiar behavior deviations of her boss need not bring up the matter to him in order for her to achieve some of her goals.

Conversely, the wise manager makes certain that his adversaries never learn where his bodies are buried, lest they be used against him at the most inopportune time. One executive made the mistake of allowing his secretary to learn of certain freedoms he was taking with his expense account. The day came when she used this knowledge to protect her job, to the embarrassment of the executive. Another man, during an hour of relaxation at a local watering hole with a peer, disclosed that he had been fired from his last job for suspicion of treating corporate finances as his own. This information found its way into the wrong ears, doing no one any good.

Rather obviously, this tactic is a dangerous one to use because there are many who will not tolerate blackmail for one instant. They fully understand the game. Once they submit to blackmail, they lose their ability to control the situation. The would-be blackmailer had better be quite sure of his victim or he may rue the day he ever thought of the tactic.

Pay 'em Off

Only the most naive manager is unaware that bribery is a fact of life in economic endeavors. Money buys a great many things—people, favors, and patronage. But bribery can take forms other than money, and many times these other forms are vastly more effective than the mere offering of funds. So when the manager resorts to dollar bribes, he leaves little room for the recipient to defend himself rationally. It is an outright, crass bribe and there is little the person can do to see it any other way.

Thus it is a wise manager who finds other means of paying off an individual. Perhaps he can bestow upon the person a new position or a meaningful gift, or grant him some favor he seeks. In any event, such bribes can be far more effective than money, because they continue to exist long after the act of giving has taken place, whereas money is pocketed, spent, and soon forgotten.

Make no mistake about it, there are times and places in which a bribe is the only tactic that will get the job done. The question faced by the executive is whether to bribe or to fail in the task. One top executive in a large oil company related his experiences in setting up operations in one Middle Eastern country;

a rather substantial number of public officials had to be bribed in many ways, including the bestowal of substantial sums of money in certain depositories located in the Alps. While the conduct of these public officials inwardly outraged the executive, he had to comply or else he would have failed in his mission and his career would most certainly have been dealt a severe blow. He was able to rationalize his behavior by saying that bribery was simply a way of life in that culture.

Let's examine some less blatant cases of the *pay 'em off* tactic. A university department head assumed his position over the vocal objections of one member of the department who was in a position to make considerable trouble for the new manager. One of the first managerial moves the new head made was to have a talk with his adversary. During the conversation he casually asked his adversary what courses he preferred to teach and during what days and hours he would like to hold classes—items dear to the hearts of most professors. Upon departure, the department head said, "I can't guarantee anything, you understand, but if all goes well I should be able to get you the schedule you want." The professor, wise to the ways of academic communications, correctly interpreted this statement as meaning, "If you are a good boy and don't make any waves you will get the schedule you want. Otherwise, set your alarm clock early and bring your supper." The professor proved to be a model of acquiescent behavior. There were no waves. He had been paid off.

A young entrepreneur who specialized in locating refreshment stands at fairs and other recreational locations had an idea for locating some ice cream stands on the beaches of one southern California town. He approached the mayor about the idea and it was suggested by His Honor that the man go see a certain lawyer who also happened to be the mayor's brother-in-law. The businessman and the lawyer met, at which time the lawyer reacted most favorably to the proposition, declaring, "That would be a great moneymaker; just has to be a winner!"

"Then you think you can arrange it?" asked the young businessman.

"Why certainly *we* can arrange it. *We* can form a separate company and go right at it. *We* can get the council's permission, I'm sure," the lawyer gushed.

The businessman, somewhat startled, replied, "I don't think you quite understand. I want to do this with my existing company. I simply want to hire your services to do it for me. I'm perfectly willing to pay you a reasonable fee for your services, but I'm not looking for any partners."

The lawyer replied, "It's you, I think, who doesn't understand. The only way I'm willing to work is on a partnership basis. I want a piece of the action or you don't get on the beaches!"

There are no ice cream stands on those beaches today, because the businessman had a firm policy of not having any partners. He wouldn't pay the lawyer off.

Perhaps you jump to the conclusion that I am criticizing the businessman for his obstinate ways, but as a matter of fact I strongly recommended that course of action to the concessionaire because he didn't need any partners. There were too many alternative opportunities open for him to become enmeshed in a case of political bribery and the potential problems entailed by such a tactic. But the point is that in that situation the only way business could be done was by paying the man off.

There are some people who claim that it is imprudent to go into business with a lawyer, because he is holding too many good cards and is in a position to cause you great difficulties if he becomes unhappy with your handling of affairs. Remember, he can sue quite cheaply and it costs you money, lots of it, to defend yourself. Moreover, rest assured that he will have all the documents you sign at the beginning of the relationship structured in his favor. Additionally, if he gets greedy and believes he no longer needs you, he may find some ways to move you out of the picture.

Let me make it quite clear right here that grave potential dangers lie waiting for bribers. The law may extract a painful penalty if, for some reason, things go wrong. There are people in prison who failed to comprehend such risks. Phil Reagan, the former singer, was convicted and imprisoned for trying to bribe a minor city official on a zoning matter. Small potatoes, you might mutter, but I doubt if he now thinks so. If you must bribe, take care because it can destroy your career.

White Hat—Black Hat

As every good Western fan knows, there are good guys and there are bad guys. The good guys wear the white hats and the bad guys wear the black hats. So it is with many negotiations. Great advantages accrue to a negotiator who can arrange to have on his side both a villain and a hero, because villains can say and do a great many things that heroes cannot and, conversely, heroes can accomplish a great many things closed off to the villain. In any business deal there are always a great many things that one would like to say to his adversaries but feels reluctant to say because it may alienate them so much that future negotiations or concessions may be cut off.

Three men were partners in a mercantile chain. Naturally, they had a great many dealings in all sorts of situations. The *white hat—black hat* maneuver was one of their favorite tactics. One of the men made a particularly convincing villain; he was the man who had the greatest technical expertise, but he also had a manner about him that was somewhat abrasive. Prior to going into negotiations the three men would agree that all of the negotiating would be done by the villain. If the heroes detected that they had pushed the adversary too far or were stepping on some particularly sensitive toes, they would come in and rebuke the villain, thus earning the gratitude of the adversary.

Police have used this tactic most successfully in wringing confessions from suspects. The villain physically and verbally browbeats the suspect, who is saved in the nick of time by the hero who gives him solace, thus earning the suspect's gratitude. Then the suspect is expected to react to his savior's plea for information. Good guy—bad guy! The bad guy can push to the limit and be most unreasonable, while the good guy maintains a liaison with and the good friendship of the adversary for future favors.

In fact, the three merchants previously referred to were so successful in using this tactic that in one instance the landlord of a shopping center pleaded over the phone, "Okay, okay, I'll give you anything you want. Just don't send that bastard down to talk to me again." He surrendered rather than having to face the villain again. The partnership had managed to create the situation in which they were tacitly telling their adversaries, "You better be good to us or we will send our bad guy in to see you."

This tactic is closely akin to using a hatchet man, in which the manager lets someone else do his evil deeds, thus mantaining his posture as a good guy.

Hitch a Lie to a Truth

One of the finer points of persuasive lying is the adroit hitching of a lie to a recognized truth or, better yet, several truths. The principle underlying this tactic should be readily apparent. If one tells the adversary several truths that he recognizes, he is more likely to believe that the lie told him is also the truth. Consider the opposite situation, in which one has lied to a person several times and then makes a true statement. How in the world will he ever believe it? This principle was illustrated in a previous section in connection with the bluffing tactic. A prospective football coach told a board of regents that he had an offer from another university (which was a recognized truth); then he said he was going to accept the offer that evening (which was a lie); but the fact that he had *hitched the lie to the truth* made it believable.

The landlord of an industrial building wanted to raise the rent on his tenant; the tenant was most reluctant to pay, preferring instead to plead poverty. Now the truth of the matter was that the landlord was quite happy with the tenant and wanted him to remain in the building; but had the tenant known this fact, he most certainly would never have agreed to an increase in his rent from $480 to $600 a month. So the landlord listed the property with a broker for sale or lease (truth 1) and served legal notice on the tenant that, as of the expiration date of the lease, he should be prepared to vacate the premises (truth 2). Now the landlord was quite certain the tenant did not want to move, because to do so would cost several thousands of dollars plus much inconvenience, so he hitched a lie to the two truths and informed the tenant that he had an offer to lease the property for $600 a month. The lease was signed immediately, because the tenant had no way of knowing that the bluff was a lie, particularly when combined with the third truth—that the market rate for the property was at least $600 a month.

Make the Future Look More Expensive

Timing is usually critical in negotiations. It is indeed difficult to get a person to agree to something that is basically disadvantageous to him, especially if he is under no pressure to do so. He must have a reason for making the settlement now, and one of the best reasons you can provide is that *the future is going to be even more expensive.* You must create the picture that by agreeing to your proposition now, no matter how expensive it will be to him, it will be significantly more expensive to delay.

One delinquent taxpayer was in no hurry at all to settle with the IRS, because he was only being charged 6 percent on the taxes due and he couldn't borrow the money for less than 9 percent elsewhere. So why not let the government finance him for 6 percent? The future was not sufficiently expensive that he was willing to settle the amount in dispute. He took the matter all the way to tax court, because he had to pay no out-of-pocket costs in so doing. He had no attorney's or accountant's fees to worry about.

The owner-manager of a small manufacturing plant was negotiating with a potential buyer over its sale. The owner wanted to sell the business for $4.5 million, while the buyer only wanted to pay $3.5 million. A million dollars is something to negotiate about. Finally the seller proposed that they split the difference down the middle and consummate the sale at $4 million, but the buyer would not readily succumb to that offer; rather he hung tough for his $3.5 million because he felt that the seller would eventually accept it. However, the seller knew that the buyer wanted the business badly and he also knew that it was an exceptionally good value at $4 million, a value that no rational person could pass up. Somehow the seller had to make waiting look expensive to the buyer. In this case, an event transpired that the seller turned to his advantage. A large customer for whom the manufacturer made a private brand contacted him to renegotiate their contract. The contract represented a potential profit of $2 million. The seller immediately contacted the potential buyer and informed him that since the new contract would be so lucrative, once it was signed he was going to withdraw his offer to sell the business for $4 million. The buyer's immediate reaction was one of disbelief, until he was shown documents verifying the potential contract. Since in his mind he already owned the concern, he quickly saw that he had better get in and actually assume management of it—and the quicker the better, because things would most likely become more expensive in the future.

Frequently the proposition is put to a person in a legal conflict that he should either settle now for a certain amount of money or settle later in court for a whole lot more. One of the basic strategies of most lawyers representing plaintiffs is to sue for a great deal of money to make the future look as expensive as possible for the defendant, thus encouraging him to settle immediately for some reasonable amount.

Salting the Mine

In the days of the Golden West it was not unknown for the owner of a worthless mine who had located a naive prospective buyer to scatter some rich ore around the premises, or perhaps load some gold dust into a shot gun and blast away at some likely quartz seam—he *"salted" the mine.*

This tactic is equally applicable to other types of sales. It would be rare to encounter a deal which includes property that has not in some way been salted—that is, made to appear to be more favorable than it is. Businessmen with enterprises to sell adeptly arrange the proper numbers in the financial statements. Certain costs are ignored or sales claimed that were not made. Indeed, it is a most difficult task to determine the true financial performance of a firm that is for sale. True, any material misrepresentation is grounds for a court suit, but clever "salters" know how to do their jobs in such a manner that proof of the salting is nearly impossible to obtain.

A small apparel merchant was trying to sell his store. When potential buyers came into the establishment they witnessed several bits of staging. The "will call" rack of altered garments recently sold was full; many sales tickets were in the cash drawer; the cash drawer was loaded; the merchant made certain that there would be some "good" customers (some friends and relatives) in the store buying impressive amounts of goods; and the phone kept ringing, ostensibly calls from customers (his wife). It was all very impressive because buyers like to see lots of action in the places they want to buy.

The owner-manager of a large collegiate tavern and dance hall was trying to sell it for $180,000; he had bought it for $130,000 a year previously. He was a master at salting his gold mine. Every time a potential buyer wanted to see the place the owner hauled out a great deal of cash from the safe (he kept it there solely as "salt") and arranged it in many stacks all over his desk. It was most impressive. Drool dripped and eyes widened as the suckers were escorted into his trap. He got $170,000 for his mine. And he got out just in time.

Few things excite a person's mind so much as gold and cash, large amounts of it. Such emotions block good judgment. Thus, one should immediately be put on his guard when an adversary exposes such wealth, because that exposure is not in itself good judgment, nor normal good business practice—you're being hustled!

The Architect's Window

An architect will labor meticulously, developing a beautiful set of plans with all of the features in harmonious relationship with one another. Then at the end he may place some god-awful feature—perhaps a window—in such a manner that it sticks out like a sore thumb. Then he takes his creation to the client who, after surveying the scene, points to the window and says, "Great god, that's awful! That's gotta come out of there!" The architect dutifully hauls out his eraser, removes the offending window, and thus allows the client to feel he has really contributed something to the plan.

Managers have been known to use the same tactic. A production manager was rearranging his plant layout for better utilization of factory space and he knew that the boys in the shop would want to participate in the redesigning. However, he wasn't about to turn the project over to a committee because he wanted to be certain that the final result was exactly as he wanted it and not just somebody else's thinking. He proceeded to draw up the plan, deliberately putting the locker room, the tool crib, and a few relatively unimportant items in inconvenient locations; but he designed his basic layout so that the items could be moved to their logical locations without disrupting any of his other plans. After he had completed his task, he turned it over to the boys in the shop for their suggestions. Their final recommendations placed the tool crib and the locker rooms and the lunch area all in the proper locations. They had removed *the architect's window*.

This tactic does carry with it a certain amount of risk. There are some clods in this world who will think the window is beautiful right where it is; you may get stuck with something you don't want. However, this risk is really minimal because the clever manager can find a way to eliminate his deficiencies afterward by creating some excuse for why the plan had to be changed again.

Set The Hook

Adept fishermen know quite well that when a fish first takes the bait they must take care to *set the hook* in the fish's mouth before trying to reel it in. Sometimes they do this by a short, sudden jerk, but if they do it too soon the fish will not have the hook in his mouth, thus escaping the angler.

The same tactic is frequently required in managerial affairs. A small entrepreneur who contracted production to various manufacturers was relatively underfinanced for the ventures he was intending to undertake. His studies indicated that he might possibly need upwards of a quarter of a million dollars to finance the production and inventory of a certain promising new product he was developing. At best this entrepreneur could raise $10,000. But lack of money seldom deters the enterprising man; where there's a will there's a way, and all of that.

In discussing working relationships with a potential new subcontractor who was very interested in the future of the product, he learned that this supplier had an excellent line of credit at the bank—upwards of a half-million dollars. Moreover, he noted that the subcontractor had just moved into new quarters and was operating considerably under capacity. The man was obviously hungry for volume. The entrepreneur plotted. He decided that his venture was going to be financed on his supplier's line of credit. It also seemed likely that a direct approach to the supplier might be more hazardous than an oblique one. The entrepreneur decided that he had better set the hook first before trying to reel in this line of credit. He first contracted for the man to do the artwork, which amounted to only $1,500 for the entire product line. This whetted the supplier's interest, because now he could see the potential for the items. Then the entrepreneur built the prototypes in order to procure some large orders from the mass merchandising institutions. He returned with some orders that presented no financial problem, so he gave the subcontractor some reasonable orders which required no unusual financing methods. The subcontractor set up his lines and started production.

Then the entrepreneur brought in a very large order, one he could not finance. He laid it down before the supplier, a firm order from a large triple-A company, and reeled in his fish. The hook had been set with the previous small order. The supplier was in production on the item and that large, additional volume was extremely appealing to him. He agreed to wait for payment until the triple-A firm paid for the order.

In many negotiations one must be exceedingly careful that he not try to close the deal until the adversary has the hook firmly set in his mouth. He has to have taken the bait.

A contrary example will illustrate. The president of one medium-sized oil company was trying to attract a particularly talented comptroller to join his organization in Los Angeles. The president made the mistake of trying to haul the man in before he had been sold on the idea of moving to Los Angeles from Houston, where he was happily living very comfortably in the River Oaks area. The comptroller was relatively unfamiliar with Los Angeles and his head was full of ideas concerning the congestion and smog.

The president made an attractive offer to the man over the phone, because he had known him for a number of years and was certain he was the man for the job. While the comptroller said he would think it over for a few days, it was highly unlikely that the frontal attack tactic would work. The hook hadn't been set. Instead, the president should have invited the man and his family to Los Angeles for several days, housed them on the ocean, and shown them the luxury that could be theirs. You've got to show the bait and get 'em to go for it—then set the hook—before the adversary can be yours.

The standard recruiting tactic for one department chairman of a university located in Orange County, California, was to bring the person into the Orange County airport rather than Los Angeles, because there a distinctly more favorable impression could be made on the person. The recruit was then housed in the Newporter Inn, a hostelry of considerable luxury, and wined and dined at some of Newport Beach's famed restaurants. Why go to all this trouble? Because all the university had to sell was climate and environment—the wages and working conditions were not attractive. So the tactic was to set the hook quickly before negotiations got around to such mundane topics as salaries and work load.

Establish Expertise Early

A long-time Washington bureaucrat disclosed that one of the favorite tactics of a high-ranking official, upon beginning an important meeting on some subject, is to make some opening statement about the topic that clearly established himself as highly knowledgeable about it. A staff assistant furnishes him with the needed information.

If you, however, come alone armed with a headful of highly selective data, you start with an enormous moral advantage. At a moment of your choosing, you will say something like this, "What bothers me is the long range effect of all this on the coal industry. It's all very well to talk about domestic fuel oil, but if you look at the probable effect of reducing the quotas on imported residual fuel oil as a function of price, you can see that by the middle 1970's 38 cents per 1,000 btu's will not even be competitive with nuclear power, let alone oil. It's obvious what that will mean to the coal industry."

Few things have been less obvious. . . . but no one at the meeting will say so.[1]

Once you have *established yourself as knowledgeable* about a subject, others are more careful about trying to run a bluff on you. Moreover, your opinions and statements will carry more weight than if your credentials are in doubt.

All of this sounds clever, but it is an extremely dangerous tactic to use because your entire career can go up in smoke if there is someone at the table who knows you are talking nonsense and is of a mind to expose you as a fraud. It's not worth the risk.

Instead, you must truly establish that you are an expert, someone who knows what he is talking about. Thus your first comments need not be long statements. A short observation that clearly shows you are an expert will do.

A retail clothing salesman would carefully observe the approaching prospect's physical characteristics and thus perceive some of the man's problems in buying well-fitting garments. Then early in the sale he would mention something about it, such as, "I see you probably have trouble with coats fitting you too tight under the arms. Let's look at a line made to fit men with big shoulders." Thus the prospect was given a suggestion that the salesman was an expert in fitting clothes. Subsequent behavior would confirm that suggestion.

Failure to establish your expertise early can be a nuisance.

[1]Will Sparks, "Who Talked To the President Last?" (New York: W. W. Norton & Company, Inc.) p. 45.

Having rather respectable golfing skills, I fell in one day at the club with some hacker with whom I had never played. For some reason known only to the god of golf I played the first hole horribly. That was a terrible mistake; I was immediately innundated with all sorts of silly suggestions on what was wrong with my swing. Silence was my refuge. At the next hole I took particular care not to repeat the debacle and that spared me further comment from my companion. I should have managed to communicate my handicap to him on the first tee, but there was no occasion because we did not bet. It would have saved considerable embarrassment—for him, not me—because he was noticeably conscious of his faux pas for the remainder of the round.

How Does the Land Lie?

A retailer spent a great deal of time and money trying to obtain the lease to a particularly good location on which he wanted to build a store. The owner proved difficult; he stalled and hemmed and hawed. After one lengthy meeting over the dinner hour, the dealer left with the feeling that the matter was wrapped up—the site was his. The next day he learned from a competitor that the location had been purchased by a large chain operation, a situation that he knew nothing about. He called the owner to inquire of the matter. "Certainly I sold it to them. It was theirs all along. All they had to do was make up their mind."

"Why didn't you tell me this from the start?" the dealer inquired.

"You didn't ask!"

Prentice-Hall trains its field editors to always ask of potential authors such questions as, "What houses have you contacted?

Are you obligated to any other publisher? Who would you like to publish your work?" Find out *how the land lies* before committing your forces. It's pointless to waste time on matters in which there are commitments that make your success unlikely.

Ask questions early in a negotiation to find out the other party's state of mind, what he is thinking about, what he wants to do. It will save you much time and chagrin later when such information pops up to block you.

6

Some Tactical Problems

and how they were handled or mishandled

Tactical Problem 1

C.C. and the Boston Shootout

Wally had worked for C.C. as second-in-command for five years with great effectiveness. Wally was good in his job and made much money for C.C. but that evidently was not sufficient for they slowly grew to dislike each other for a variety of irrelevant reasons. Among Wally's customer's was one large Boston concern whose orders accounted for 20 percent of C.C.'s total sales volume. The Boston customer was most impressed with Wally's talents. Thus, it came to pass that they made Wally an offer he couldn't refuse: to take full charge of the operations that were buying from C.C.'s concern. Now Wally was C.C.'s customer, a development that C.C. could not accept gracefully and one he set out to reverse.

C.C. was trying to renew the contract on one item in particular but was being rebuffed by Wally who intended to buy that item elsewhere. The article was being purchased for a 33 percent discount from list but Wally was now getting a 50 percent discount from a new source. C.C. did not want to meet prices but instead had notified the Boston management that all prices were being increased. That did not go over very well to say the least.

When it became clear that C.C. was about to lose the business he called Wally's boss and asked to meet with him. He replied, "Wally is in full charge of that operation. See him!"

C.C. replied, "No, I want to see you."

The boss finally relented and agreed to a meeting with C.C. five days hence—Tuesday.

Question
As Wally's boss what do you now do?

The Follow Up

Wally's boss immediately got Wally on the phone in Los Angeles and said, "Get your ass here Tuesday morning. You have a customer to talk with." And then he filled in Wally with all the details. They backed him all the way.

Now that is a real boss. They were not going to allow C.C. to try a divide and conquer. There are many times you do not want to hear what someone says without the proper people in attendance.

C.C. walked into the Boston office that Tuesday morning and was shocked to say the least. He tried to protest but was sharply cut off with, "We told you, C.C., that Wally is running that operation and we meant it. We are completely happy with how Wally is doing and if you cannot do business with him that is your problem. Quit trying to make it ours."

C.C. used dismally bad tactics because he grossly misjudged his adversary's power with his new employers. Wally had made them more than $500,000 during his first month of employment.

C.C. did not comprehend that his best tactic would have been to try to make peace with Wally and have Wally tell him what it was going to take to do business.

Tactical Problem 2

Charles and the Runaway Committee

Charles was the dean of a large engineering school whose power had been waning in recent months to the point where the university's top administration had placed another person into a position to run the internal operations of the school. Charles had instituted certain programs that reflected his unique educational philosophy. These programs were at odds with what 90 percent of Charles' faculty deemed desirable. Charles had been able to have his programs activated previously because of his unusual power base, a power base that had recently evaporated because he had failed to deliver on most of his promises of revenue. However, he still felt strongly about his programs.

The new administration had elected a curriculum committee whose charge it was to review the school's whole program with an eye to some substantial changes. Charles was apprehensive. He asked to appear before the committee to present his "case" and was so invited. As one committee member later observed, "It was embarrassing." The committee turned an icy shoulder to Charles and his ideals. They were not buying them any longer. He saw that his position was weakening so he sought outside aid. He asked that the committee hear another dean whose national credentials were impressive; he felt this other dean would support his position and thus persuade the committee to keep its hands off of his program. The committee really didn't want to hear what this other dean had to say because as one member put it, "He sits up in the tower in his school and we sit down here in ours and the two are completely different. He knows little about our problems and our students."

Nevertheless, the committee felt that politics required that the esteemed dean be invited in and so the date was set: March 15. Yet the committee felt that it was being outmaneuvered—the adversary was bringing in "an Expert."

Question
What if anything does the committee do to protect itself from the dean's "expert"?

The Follow Up

The committee invited its own "expert": another dean with equally suitable credentials whose philosophies were known to be roughly the same as those of the committee's. More importantly, the committee's expert was invited to appear prior to the dean's expert. The committee wanted to make certain that it had its support in hand when the dean's proponent came before it.

Even more forceful, the committee instituted efforts to indirectly convey to the dean's expert that he was sticking his nose into one hell of a faculty fight and might not want it bloodied. Since it would be natural for the dean to have told only his side of the story to his expert, the thought was that perhaps the expert's testimony would be tempered somewhat if he was in possession of the opposition's attitudes.

Tactical Problem 3

Rickie—An Insecure Employee

Ross, the boss, was talking casually one morning to Mose, an overly excitable yet useful subordinate who could be relied upon to furnish at least three items of organizational gossip each day. The day's message was, "Rickie is getting restless and looking for a low place in the fence to jump."

"You must be kidding me," was Ross' reply.

"I'm deadly serious. He's looking around and not just for fun."

"Why he's one of my best men. I'm putting him up for promotion this time around."

"I know that but he is still afraid that he's pulling on the hind one," Mose insisted.

"Why? What reason could he have?" Ross inquired.

"He sees himself as low man on the totem pole around here and thinks that when the dust settles he will be left holding the bag right where he is. After all, look at his three competitors in your operation. Bob is a sure winner; he is so locked-in politically around here. Jim is a friend of yours and Hal has seniority," Mose itemized.

"Well, thanks for the information. I'll have to get on it because Rickie is one of my best men," Ross confessed. He made such a statement knowing full well that in many managerial circles such a judgement could easily come back to haunt him as the other three would certainly hear of it. However, he knew that the message would get back to Rickie and that was what he wanted.

Question
What should Ross do, if anything, about Rickie's insecurity? Was he wise in telling Mose so much?

The Follow Up

Ross immediately got on the telephone after Mose left the office to call Rickie.

"Are you going to be coming by my office any time soon?" he inquired.

"As a matter of fact I was headed that way right now," was Rickie's reply.

"Drop in when you get here," Ross asked.

Rickie entered the office and was invited to sit down in the overstuffed chair in the corner ensemble and was joined by Ross.

"I hear from the jungle tom-toms that you are not feeling too secure here. Is that right?" Ross asked.

"Well, I'll tell you, Ross, I do have some strong fears."

So the two talked at length about Rickie's situation during which Ross clearly conveyed his own high opinions of Rickie's work.

It was one-on-one, honest and straightforward. For support Ross asked his boss to join the meeting about midway through it in order to add still another evaluation to the picture.

Note the tactics—speed, one-on-one, honesty, and use of outside authority.

Tactical Problem 4

Dan

Tom did not like some of the things he had been seeing recently. He had hired a young man of great promise, Dan, and had grown to like him. They did things socially and were most compatible. But lately he noted that Dan, a bachelor, had been drinking alone. He would be well-lubricated at the beginning of the evening and then proceed to put down double martinis at twice the rate of others in the group until the ultimate state of intoxication would be reached. Dan had insisted on driving home one night over Tom's observations that he should let his companion drive. It was not a wise decision. Moreover, Dan was dating one of his secretaries; a mistake in Tom's book.

Tom grieved over the situation for he hated to see this happening to his friend. He sought advice from some other executives for whom he held respect. He got three different opinions:

1. A colleague thought it best not to confront Dan directly about the matter but try to have one of Dan's peers drop a few hints in his ear.

2. A friend who headed another business said emphatically, "Face him with it directly and don't spare the words. It's the only way to deal with an alcoholic. Hints will go right over his head."

3. A mutual friend said, "Don't do anything. It's none of your business yet since it hasn't affected his work. When he does something tangibly wrong on the job then it becomes your business."

"But don't I have any obligation to Dan as a friend?" Tom asked the mutual friend.

"You take you friends as you find them. It's not your privilege under the guise of friendship to try to reform Dan. Dan is Dan. Take him as he is or forget him but in any case leave him alone," was the friend's reply.

Question
What, if anything, would you do?

The Follow Up

Tom did nothing. He finally concluded that he had to let the situation worsen before he could act, otherwise, it would appear that he was a teetotaling meddler. He quietly probed into Dan's life and found that there were some problems causing the behavior. Dan was under great pressure in his job because one project was having difficulty. Moreover, he was having little success with his social life. Tom decided he would wait to see if those problems would abate and, thus, relieve Dan's need for drink.

There are respected tacticians who insist that Tom's decision was really based on his friendship for Dan and not upon a rational appraisal of what he should do as Dan's boss. Many administrators insist that Dan's behavior is Tom's business and that to ignore the situation does no one any good. Thus the dangers of being friends with one's subordinates becomes apparent.

Tactical Problem 5

The Lease

Shopco, a large developer of regional shopping malls, sought as a tenant in its new mall, Teen Shop, a small specialty store with a highly esteemed local reputation. The Teen Shop was an outstanding merchandising operation. Its management was not inclined to expand into Shopco Mall until it was given an attractive lease which included, among other things, an allowance of $40,000 for completing the concrete shell into the finished Teen Shop. Another clause said that Shopco would not lease space to any other store carrying any of the Teen Store's major brands of goods, all of which were listed in the lease. Matters proceeded normally until one day Shopco management called Roy, the owner of the Teen Shop.

"Say we're going to have to ask you to release us from that exclusive line clause in the lease. We are trying to lease to Mode Shops and they carry many of the same lines. We need them."

Roy was stunned but reacted, "That's all well and good but I see no reason for us to change that lease. We're happy with it. As I recall, all bets are made on the first tee box."

"Well, Roy, read your lease. It says that if we do not notify you that your shell is ready for your completion within three years, the lease is null and void. We can just let your space sit there for three years and forget you while Mode Shops does all that business." Shopco stated with firmness.

"I have read that lease and I know what you say is true." Roy replied.

Question
Now what does Roy do?

The Follow Up (a)

Roy was no fool. He knew damn good and well that no shopping center developer could let his key space sit empty for three years. It was a bluff. Moreover, Roy did not really care; he was willing to walk out the door at anytime. So he said, "That's fine. You do what you think you have to do but we'll not agree to any change in the lease."

A few days later Roy had another call from Shopco. "We have decided to let Mode Shops into the mall and if you don't like it then you will just have to sue us."

Roy now knew they were truly desperate to try such an obviously shabby bluff as this because no landlord could stand such a suit in the beginning stages of trying to lease a center. Moreover, the mortgage holder would not look with favor upon such nonsense. And to top it off Roy knew just enough law to know that he could embroil Mode Shops in the suit also. Roy was a good merchant and knew that it was most unlikely that Mode Shops management wanted any part of a suit for they could be charged with third party interference with a contract.

Question
What does Roy say?

Follow Up (b)

Roy said, "I guess that I'll be seeing you and Mode Shops in court." And he hung up.

Five minutes later another phone call reopened the matter.

The caller was not the same person who had been making all the loud threats. Now the tone had changed. "Ok, Roy, what do we do to settle this thing?"

Question
What does Roy say?

Follow Up (c)

"How about talking money?" Roy replied.

"What do you mean money?"

"You know green stuff, coin of the realm, moola, dough, whatever you call it. If you want that clause back you'll have to buy it. The price is another $30,000 in finishing allowances."

"We can't do that. That is ridiculous! Be reasonable!" was the reply.

"I think I was reasonable to begin with. Just let the lease alone. You're the guy who wants to change it." Roy said.

"Well, forget it." And the conversation ended. Roy had tried the quid pro quo but had been rejected.

Question
Now what does Roy do?

Follow Up (d)

Nothing! Absolutely nothing! The ball is in their court. Roy is holding aces back to back. He let them come to him. And they did. Two hours later they were back.

"Will you take $5000?"

"No. The price is $30,000."

"There is no way we can do that. Believe me. The very best we can do is another $15,000 and that is generous."

It so happened that the extra money would allow Roy to build the store without any investment on his part so he accepted the offer. Quid pro quo.

Tactical Problem 6

The Two Bosses

A large consumer goods concern encountered some problems which resulted in the resignation of the person who was in charge of operations. The big boss who had been devoting himself exclusively to "statesmanship" activities throughout the world was forced to either hire a new operations manager or take over operational control himself. The organization had no one in it who was acceptable to the big boss as an operational head. Yet the organization was experiencing a crisis which demanded strong leadership of the troops. The board of directors recognized the need for such leadership and, thus, demanded of the statesman his return to the helm.

He came before the board and said, "I have given intense and considerable thought to our problem and to my career and have decided that I just am not at all interested in doing all the things that an operational manager does. I want to continue to do all the things that I have been doing on the national scene for our organization. So I propose to step aside and let you appoint an executive vice-president to run the company while I continue my work for us with the outside agencies."

Since he had developed a national reputation, the board accepted the offer and kept him as president while appointing Roger, one of the company's two senior vice-presidents, as executive vice-president. Moreover, it took the unusual step of instructing Roger to report directly to the board and not to the President. Even more importantly, the board gave Roger full and complete control over operations. "You have the full powers of the president in everything but name."

Things started happening in the organization all for the good, or so most people thought, for many of the firm's problems were being attacked. Things were humming, but suddenly the "statesman" saw some things that displeased him. He came down and began acting like a president much to the consternation of everyone. The people suddenly found that they had two bosses. The executive vice-president complained to some confidants on the board but was told to be patient and that everything would work out alright when the statesman found other work. He just had not been able to make other connections yet and the board did not want to embarrass him by any direct confrontation at that time. In the meantime, the organization was growing disenchanted with the executive vice-president for it appeared to them that he lacked courage and leadership. "If he has the power, why doesn't he use it?" was a question one could hear at the coffee pot at any time during the day. "Who is running this company?" was its companion question.

The board had assured the executive vice-president that everything would be solved within two weeks but declined to provide details. His subordinates kept after him but he would beg off, "Trust me. Everything will work out in two weeks. Just give me two weeks." While they had to grant such a deferral, they were not happy for the statesman was causing problems each day. He would not stay "outside".

Question

What should the executive vice-president do?

The Follow Up

While several of the VP's subordinates urged him to make a direct frontal attack on the adversary by presenting the board with a "it's him or me" ultimatum, he chose a Fabian bob and weave tactic. Avoid confrontations. Let the statesman come in and mess up operations because with each attempt at operational control he looked even more pathetic; he was destroying himself. The VP decided to let the man ruin himself. Any damage to the organization could later be remedied, or so he thought, and the board would only have itself to blame. In any event, he was of the opinion that any direct frontal assault on the board would be defeated. Such men do not react favorably to such direct pressure and were apt to sweep out the VP as well as the President. Let the situation worsen was combined with Let him furnish his own rope.

Tactical Problem 7

Settling Debts

Billy had been assigned the unpleasant job of trying to keep a small business out of bankruptcy court while closing it down. The business owed about $40,000 but had only $15,000 cash after sale of assets with which to pay those debts. The creditors numbered about twenty, some of whom were local organizations while others were national concerns. Each situation was different. The lawyer had instructed him to write a letter to each creditor offering a settlement of 37 percent. Some of Billy's associates thought that was a bit troublesome and unnecessary inasmuch as the company was clearly broke and there was little for anyone to grab if they went to court. Any filing of bankruptcy would result in the creditors getting little if anything because the $15,000 would then be given to the lawyers who handled the bankruptcy. That's the way those things work. While he wasn't too afraid of court, still there was good reason to try to settle up many of the debts. Court could cause trouble by tying up the assets that had been sold. It could be a mess.

Question
How should Billy handle the matter?

The Follow Up

Billy made a list of all the creditors and how much they were owed. Then he evaluated each item as to:

Their ability to make trouble.
Their freedom to compromise debts.
Their actual dollar investments in the debt.
Their attitudes.

Firms that were owed relatively small amounts and that were located in distant towns with no local representatives were ignored. Forget them, they can't cause trouble because it would cost more than it would be worth.

Two local concerns that had been particularly helpful and that were owed substantial sums were to be offered substantial settlements.

Coca-Cola was ignored. It had made a lot of money from the operation and was only owed $400. It's actual dollar investment in the syrup sold was not more than $40. It was not likely that they would do anything.

And so it went. Each creditor was appraised and separate tactics were developed.

Then Billy went to the bank and withdrew the $15,000 in cash, $100 bills. He then would walk into the creditor's office with the statement of account. The telephone company serves as an example; it was owed $430. Billy laid out a $100 dollar bill and said, "This is your share of what is left of the company. You want to settle our debt for it?" In all but two cases, the executive took the money and signed the bill paid in full. The electric company, which was owed $900 and had been offered two hundred to settle, refused, "Company policy will not allow us to settle debts if the customer has not declared bankruptcy" was the pompous reply. So the power company got absolutely nothing.

A paper wholesaler who was owed $400 refused to go along on advice of an eager lawyer who claimed he could get the whole amount in court. He sued and got nothing; he made some bad tactical errors in trying to sue the officers of the corporation personally for the debt and was unable to panic them into paying up because they were confident he could not pierce the corporate shield. The lawyer waltzed them to the court house steps but lost his bluff when it was called.

All the others grabbed the money and ran; they knew a good deal when they saw it.

Tactical Problem 8

The Fence

Harry wanted a sharp looking swimming pool area so he had decided that a wrought iron fence around the pool would be just the thing. He shopped around carefully and discovered that most fence contractors wanted around $1900 to do the job. However, one contractor that was featured in the Yellow Pages gave him a bid of $1000. The deal was set; the contractor would be out to put up the fence on the day the pool contractor was ready to pour the decking around the pool. The contract called for 50 percent down payment with the balance due upon completion.

When asked why the advance payment was needed, the contractor replied, "I need the money to buy the iron. I must make up the panels ahead of time."

Question
Should Harry sign the contract and give the advance payment?

The Follow Up

This one is really too easy, but, sorry to relate, Harry blew the whole thing. He was swindled. The guy took his $500 and left the state after a few months and a few grand jury indictments.

Always keep a hold on your money. Keep ahead of your suppliers. Under no circumstances should you allow an unknown party to get so far ahead of you that it hardly pays him to do the job.

Tactical Problem 9

The Major League Tryout

Your eighteen-year-old son, who is your pride and joy, has fulfilled your boyhood dreams of becoming a baseball star. He has just received a telephone call from the Texas Rangers' front office inviting him to come to Dallas for a tryout with the team. Although the season has been underway for two months, the Rangers' scouts have urged them to ask your son to come down, at their expense, for a look-see.

Your son asks you what he should do as it will cause him to miss a week of school. Moreover, he is not all that enthralled with the Texas Rangers. He has had the Dodgers or the Reds in mind. While they have invited both you and your son to Dallas, there is a question in your mind if you should go along as it might distract your son in some way thus jeopardizing his career.

Question
What should you do? Why?

The Follow Up

This advice comes from a famous major league manager and deserves careful thought. He maintains that both you and your son should stay home. Do not go to a major league team for such a short one-time tryout. There are several aspects of the situation to keep in mind. First, if your son is really all that good his not going to Texas for the tryout will in no way jeopardize his future in baseball nor will it lessen the Rangers' desire to see him. In fact, it may even enhance their eagerness to look at the boy.

It takes someone of great confidence in his abilities to be somewhat passive in the negotiating procedure. So do not think for one minute that a refusal to go to Dallas for a tryout will end matters there and then.

Second, and even more important, such a tryout can be disastrous for several reasons. Everyone has off days. Errors are always possible. Your son could go down there and have a bad day and that would hurt his future. The front office boys would shake their heads and cross him off their list with some nasty words about the acumen of their scout. Be assured that there is no way he can really be given enough time to really display his skills; he will only be able to show a small sample at best and if that sample is not indicative of his potentialities the tryout will prove unfortunate.

Third, he may hurt himself. Visualize the scene for a moment. Your son is sitting around the dugout waiting for attention because the manager has some other things to do. Suddenly he whirls and says "Hey kid, go out there and do your thing. Show me your stuff."

Eager to please, he is apt to rush out and throw or run with too much vigor and without proper warmup. Pop, goes his chances.

No, if they want to see your son play then let them see him perform against his peers in his own environment. Moreover, make certain he has enough time to show his skills and is not on for a one-shot look-see.

It's tough to make such decisions for every instinct, every desire, makes one want to pack his bags and go show the big boys what he is made of. But such tactics should be avoided. Show your skills on your terms—not the other fellows'.

Tactical Problem 10

High Draft Choice for Green Bay

Dan Grim, a stellar performer for the University of Colorado football team in the early 1960s, provided this tale of tactical uncertainty.

He was a high draft choice, second round as I recall, of the old Green Bay Packer Lombardi regime. Shortly after the draft was announced he received a phone call which went something like this:

"Hello, kid. I'm so-and-so from the Packers. I am flying through Denver and between planes for a couple of hours. Thought I might as well see you and give you your contract so you won't have to worry about it any more. I have our standard one right here with me. Come on down to the airport and let's have a big steak and talk about next fall and the Packers."

Dan was taken back somewhat by this approach but he reacted, "Well, how much bonus money is there and what's the salary?"

"Don't worry, kid, we give you the standard bonus and salary that we give all rookies. We treat everybody the same. Come on down and I'll go over it."

Dan did not like what he was hearing for he had been entertaining visions of greenbacks in his pockets. But he persisted. "Ok, ok, just how much is it? Talk dollars."

"Kid, not over the phone. We don't talk about such things over the phone. Come on down."

"Look, I don't want to waste my time going to Denver if we

aren't talking about the same kind of money. What are the figures?"

"Ok. The standard bonus is $500 for signing and $10,000 a year if you make the team."

Dan was shocked. He had been hearing about the big bonuses that were being given and he needed the money. $500 was nothing. He made his opinions of those figures known to the caller who replied, "Look kid. Let's get one thing straight. I couldn't care less whether or not you play with Green Bay or sign with whoever, but Green Bay doesn't need to pay all those ridiculous bonuses the newspapers write about. Most of those stories are a lot of bullshit anyway told by players to make themselves look more valuable than they really are. Now if you want to play for the World Champion Green Bay Packers you haul your ass down here and sign this contract or forget it. When I get on that plane that is the last you'll hear from us. You can just forget a pro career."

Question
What would you have done? What did Dan do? Why?

The Follow Up

Dan was shattered, his mind was reeling. He wanted in the worse way to play for Green Bay. He wanted to sign a contract. He needed the money. However, he later recalled, "All that kept me together was one single thought that for some reason popped into my head while that son-of-a-bitch was talking. They drafted me high so they must really want me. They don't waste top draft choices on dog meat. I kept saying that over and over to myself as he kept putting me down. They must want me, they must want me.

"When that no good bastard hung up I was in tears. Really torn up! I couldn't tell you what or how I suffered the next few hours until the phone rang again. It was him again with his line of bullshit. 'Kid, I missed the plane back'nome and have to stay over night. Can I come up and see you?' "

The story goes on at some length because the Green Bay man was one tough son of a bitch. But so was Dan. He got the bonus he wanted and a good contract. But only because he did not fall into the tactical trap of believing anything the other man said. It might be added that the negotiator left town twice and the whole procedure took more than a month. It was a tough deal.

Dan's basic instincts kept the other fellow from using hurry hurry on him. Anytime the other party is in such a big rush to do something that is important to you, start looking for the door. Don't be stampeded.

Tactical Problem 11

The Lure

Karen had been shopping for a new color TV set for several weeks when she happened to stop by the store of a large appliance chain operation. Since she had made up her mind about which set she really wanted and was shopping for the best price on it, she directly asked for the price of Zenith's 23-inch remote control console set. She had already been quoted a price of $740 for it at another dealership.

The salesman greeted her quite nicely and promptly said, "I'll have to look it up in the book. Come this way."

They went back to a small office in the rear of the showroom where the salesman pulled out a Zenith catalog. He looked at the price sheet with Karen looking on and found the model. As he moved his finger across the page to the price, Karen noticed that he made an error and gave her the price of the model just above the one she requested; it was $630. The salesman then took out an order pad and said, "Can I write up your order for $630 dollars?"

Karen jumped at the low price and agreed to buy so he filled out the order and had her sign it. He then said, "I'll have to get the boss' signature on it to make it all legal. Pardon me."

Within two minutes he came back at a brisk pace exclaiming, "The boss says that I must have made a mistake. The price just can't be this low on this model. He wants me to look it up again."

Karen held her breath while the salesman looked up the price and discovered his error. He shook his head and said, "I am terribly sorry but I seem to have made a bad mistake in looking up the price. Must need glasses or something. It is $750."

With that declaration he crossed out the previous price on the order sheet and wrote in $750. He then said, "Now maybe the boss will give his ok." Karen was uncertain about what to do.

Question

How should Karen handle this situation?

The Follow Up

Karen was being taken on an old tactic known as the lure in which the victim is enticed into signing some sort of document or agreeing to something because of some deliberate error that has been made in the negotiations. Knowing full well that the other party is aware of the error and is trying to take advantage of the situation, the perpetrator of this tactic hopes that the victim will go along with the new deal out of guilt and confusion.

But Karen was not having any part of the scam. She quietly got up and walked out of the store. She felt it unwise to even try to do business with any merchant so unethical and she was correct. Don't try to do business with crooks. You can't win at their game.